The
1st Book of
Ethiopian Maccabees
(*Meqabyan I*)

Translated from the text original Amharic Orthodox
Bible, with additional commentary
by: D.P. Curtin

Edited by Jessica Curtin

Library of Congress Cataloging-in-Publication Data

Copyright © 2018 Dalcassian Publishing Co.
In association with St. Macartan Press
All rights reserved.

ISBN: 1727861965
ISBN-13: 978-1727861969

Dalcassian Publishing Co.
Philadelphia PA

Dedicated to the Memory of:
Fr. Thomas F. Martin, OSA

These are the acts of [the sons of] Meqabyan spoken about the kingdom of Moabites and Midianites[1].

Chapter I
The Idolatry of the King

1:1   A certain man named Tseerutsaydan[2] loved his sin. He would often boast of the great profusion of his troops and of the great armies which he held governance over.

1:2   He had countless priests who served the false gods which he worshiped, and [he would often] bow to them and make sacrifices by night and day.

1:3   In the sightlessness of his own heart, he believed that they granted him power and strength.

1:4   He believed that they gave him sovereignty over the nations.

1:5   And as his sway over the nations progressed, he believed that [these false gods] granted him the right to supremacy.

1:6   [The King] would offer sacrifices to them by night and day,

1:7   appointing priests to serve these idols.

1:8   These priests ate from the unclean sacrifices, all the while telling the king that the idols had consumed what was offered.

1:9   They sought to proselytize among the people, so that they might make greater sacrifices to be consumed.

1:10   The king trusted in these idols, which can grant no favors, nor yield any merit to his welfare.

1:11   At the time, when his heart was blind to the truth, [the king] believed that they had given him to fate, by placing him with a diadem. It would appear to him that [these idols] had created him, for Satan[3] blocked him from knowledge of the true God, who alone grants eternal life. Rather, [Satan] sought to bring him away from life, into the fire of Gehenna[4] forever, for he believed the idols to be gods,

---

[1] Why these two specific nations from the Hebrew scriptures are selected is unknown. However, they both also appear in the Kebra Nagast (74, 78), wherein other neighbors of the historic kingdom of Israel do not.

[2] This name is a curiosity, as ordinarily the Maccabee revolt is associated with the Seleucid king, Antiochus IV Epiphanius, who is otherwise unmentioned in this text. The meaning of this name is a subject of debate. It has been suggested that this name appears to represent the folk memory of the tyrant. Some coinage from his reign give his dual capital cities and are noted with the inscription "Tyre and Sidon", which appears to constitute the transliteration of this name into Ge'ez, and later Amharic. This would also account for the pairing of these two Punic cities later in the text. Alternatively, since the Ethiopian Synaxarion calls that nation of Syria 'Saranin' (Tahisas 29), This name could also be a cognate for the 'King of Syria'.

[3] This characterization of Satan, as a misleader, trickster and rival to God, is distinctive part of Christian theology, particularly as it appears in the works of the Church Fathers starting in the 3rd century. If the section of the text that tell of the sojourn of the brothers Is of Jewish origin, then this is a later addition.

[4] The usage of the term "Gehenna" early in this text offers a potential clue to its dating, as this is a term that is found in the Hebrew Scriptures, but it not used in this association. Rabbinical literature and the Greek New Testament do utilize this word in association with a state of suffer required for final atonement following death. Its use in the Greek New Testament is extensive (Matt. 5:22, 29-30, 10;28, 18:9, 23:22; Mark 9:43, 45, 47; Luke 12:5; Jam. 3:6) and linked to more familiar notions of Hell.

1:12   but since they do not truly live, they cannot give life.

1:13   It was Satan's tyranny that misled them, which was found within their idolatry. He gave of them false speech, and said he would reveal great truths to them, and for this he was loved. [Therefore, Satan] cast the people's discernment upon the false gods and those that believe in them, and among all the children of Adam, whose prayers had become like that of the dust.

1:14   They gazed upon [the idols] in solemn reverence, and [Satan] filled their mind with their own desires. And the people complied, offering as sacrifice their young girls and young boys, children of their own blood. They spilled the innocent blood of their children.

1:15   This did not concern [the king], for Satan had savored the sacrifices he made to his gods to complete his malicious designs. [Satan sought to] bring him down into Gehenna, where he dwells, and where there is no respite for all eternity, and where all will receive chastisement.

1:16   This king, Tseerutsaydan, was full of conceit; for he had fifty idols made of false gods, and twenty idols of false goddesses.

1:17   He would often boast about his idolatry and offered glorification and praise to the idols while he made his daily sacrifices.

1:18   He commanded the people, that they too might make sacrifices to these idols. [The king] would eat from these unclean sacrifices, and ordered that the people do the same, to spread the evil which he created.

1:19   Now, [the king] had five workshops which were under his command, where he forged the idols out of iron, brass and lead.

1:20   The king had them adorned in silver and in gold, and had veiled curtains around his palaces for them, each hidden in a tabernacle.

1:21   He appointed guardians for their care and would make offerings of meat to these idols from forty creatures- ten fattened oxen and ten fatted ewes, ten barren calves and ten barren goats, along with winged birds of the air.

1:22   It appeared to [the king] that these idols ate and drank, consuming fifty bunches of grapes and fifty dishes of bread kneaded with oil.

1:23   The king said to the priests, "Take this, give it to them. Let my gods consume the meat that has been slaughtered on their account. Make them drink from of the wine I have given to them. If this is not enough to quench their desire, I will give them more."

1:24   [The king] then ordered that everyone should eat and drink from that defiling sacrifice.

1:25   He then, in his corruption, sent out his armies to march on all the nations of his realm[5], to find one who would neither make sacrifices, nor prostrate themselves [before the idols], so that they could be brought before him. He sought to punish them by fire and by sword, [for he feared that the gods] might seize his wealth and burn his palaces. [The

---

[5] See Dan. 3:4-5

king] lived in terror that they might remove his great fortune and destroy him.

1:26 "My gods are generous and great, and out of their benevolence I have forged them. Therefore, I will give chastisement on him that does not worship my gods and make sacrifices to them.

1:27 I will show punishment and retribution! For they have created the heavens and the earth, the great wide sea, the moon and sun, the rains and the wind, and all that abide in this world.

1:28 Those who will not worship shall be punished under the penalty of law, and I shall have no mercy."

Chapter II
The Sons of Meqabyan

2:1 In the lands of the tribe of Benjamin⁶, a certain man named Maccabeus was born.

2:2 He had three sons⁷, who were renowned for their warrior cunning and handsomeness.

2:3 These sons were beloved among the all the inhabitants of the empire that Tseerutsayden held sovereignty over, from Media to Midian.

2:4 The servants of the king found them, and said "Why do you bow to the gods of the king? Or offer sacrifices to them? If you refuse this, we will be forced to arrest you. You will

be taken before the king and we will seize your wealth and property, as it has been ordered by our lord."

2:5 These beautiful young boys responded, saying "The Father, Our Creator, is to whom we bow, the Maker of the heavens and of the earth. Within Him lie all things, the sea, the moon, the sun and the stars, and the heavens.

2:6 He is the true God, whom we have faith in and whom we worship."

2:7 They servants of the king were four in total, and their servant-arms bears who carried shields and spears, numbering a hundred.

2:8 They looked to capture the holy ones, but the youths escaped from their grasp unharmed.

2:9 Since these youths were skilled warriors, they raided the weapons [of the king's soldiers].

2:10 There was one among them who had fame for strangling

---

⁶ The selection of the tribal territory of Benjamin as a homeland suggests that this story recounts a different band of Jewish insurrectionist from those known in the elsewhere (1 Macc. 2:1-5)

⁷ The Ethiopian Synaxarion (Tahisas 25) offers a confused account regarding the number of brothers, stating that there are three or five at different points. However, both accounts only give names for these three.

panthers[8], throttling them like they were chickens[9].

2:11 Another of the youths killed lions with a single stone, or by striking them with the branch of a tree.

2:12 Yet another of the youths, had killed a hundred men in battle with his own sword.

2:13 [The brothers] derived their famous name from this, as it was known to all the nations from Babylonia to Moab[10].

2:14 Since they were great warriors, they were beloved by many for the features of their continence was beautiful.

2:15 Yet, because they worshipped the Lord, and had no fear of death, their beauty was derived from their wisdom, which is above all things.

2:16 These youths frightened the armies [of the king], so that there was no one skilled enough to procure their capture.

2:17 They escaped to the heights of the mountains, while the armies [of the king] returned to their cities, locking the gates of their fortresses.

2:18 [The king's soldiers] struck fear in the hearts of the people, saying "Bring forth the Meqabyans, those warriors, or we will cast fire upon your city. We will send them [as hostages] to our king, while we destroy your nation".

2:19 The people of the nation, rich and poor alike, men and women, orphans and widows, all shouted together in unison as they faced the mountains and said, "Please, do not harm us, and do not show any hostility to our nation."

2:20 They wept together and feared the wrath of the Lord. Turning to the east, they stretched out their hands and prayed to the Lord, saying "Lord, should we oppose those who seek to destroy your law and your sovereignty?

2:21 [The king] believes in objects of silver and gold, and in the hewn objects made of stone and wood. We do not wish to hear the edicts of this sinner[11], who does not hold true to your law.

2:22 He thinks himself a god, like the One who created him, but

---

[8] This is an extraordinary reference, not found elsewhere in apocryphal writings. Here we are told the name of one of the brother in its original Greek form "πανθήρα" (Panthera). Within the context of this folktale it is perhaps meaningless, but it has larger implications, as this is the name attributed either to the myth of the biological father of Christ by pagan and Jewish polemists, or conversely, to a previously unknown ancestor of Christ noted by the church fathers. Jewish sources make reference to this figure of Panthera frequently in rabbinical literature (Rosefta Hullin, 2:22f; Shabboth, 14:4/13; Qohelet Rabbah, 1:8; Abodah Zarah, 27b; Shabboth 14:4/8). The Church Father, Origen, makes reference to the meaning of this name when he quotes the pagan philosopher Celsus "'the mother of Jesus' is described as having been 'turned out by the carpenter who was betrothed to her, as she had been convicted of adultery and had a child by a certain soldier named Panthera" (Contra Celsum, 1.32) The Church Father Epiphanius offers the

alternative interpretation, that this was a name that belonged to an ancestor of Christ, named Jacob the father of Joseph (Panarion, 78.7.5), and therefore was part of his familial surname passed down generationally. The account given here appears to verify the claim of Epiphanius regarding the origin of the name, however it confuses the personage. This Panthera must have lived a century before Epiphanius' projected timeframe for Jacob. However, it seems reasonable to assume that this remained a family name as part of a now forgotten folk tradition of Christ's family.

[9] While this account is repeated in the Ethiopian Synaxarion (Tahisas 25), in that hagiography it is said that it was bears that are strangled.

[10] This combination of these two nations is unclear. Moreover, Moab as a political and cultural entity was non-existent during the revolt against the Seleucid king., having been deported by the Babylonians centuries earlier (Jer. 48)

[11] See John 9:31

You are the Lord, the Creator, who gives life and takes it.

2:23 This man, [the king], spills the blood of men and eats their flesh[12]. We do not wish to see the face of this transgressor, nor do we wish to listen to his words".

2:24 The people continued, "Yet, if it is Your will, we will go over to his camp, as we have faith in your word[13]. We will go over and let our bodies be consumed by death.

2:25 The king has said 'make sacrifices to my gods'- but we do not wish to listen to the words of this sinner.

2:26 We believe in you, Lord, that you examine the heart and minds of all men.

2:27 God of our fathers, Abraham, Isaac, and Jacob, who did your will and obeyed your law, you see the thoughts of all mankind, helping with sinner and the righteous alike.

2:28 There is nothing that can be hidden from You. Those that look to be hidden, can only be exposed by You.

2:29 We have no other God apart from You[14].

2:30 Be a rock and a foundation, shelter us in this task, that we may continue to serve You, that we might give our bodies

over to death for the sake of Your glorified name[15].

2:31 Remember [Lord], when Israel entered the land of Egypt, when you heard Jacob's prayer which glorified You. We beseech You."

2:32 Two of these handsome youths then [suddenly] stood before them.

2:33 Swords of fire[16] appeared, which crashed down like the great terror of lightning, cutting the heads off [of the youths] and killing them.

2:34 Yet, they arose from this, appearing as they had formerly. Their features again became even more handsome and they shone like the sun.

Chapter III:[17]
The Brothers are Captured

3:1 As you see before you[18], the servants of the Most High God: Abya[19], Seela[20] and Pantos[21], who died and rose again. You have seen this so that you might do likewise, rising after death, and so your continence shall shine forth like the sun in the Kingdom of Heaven.

---

[12] Besides for being overtly cannibalistic, this is a reference to the prohibition on consuming blood under Mosaic law (Lev. 17:14; Deut. 12:23). However, it is almost assuredly hyperbole.

[13] This is perhaps in reference to a number of Jews who have already adopted Greek customs and practices and become apostate to the traditional Jewish community in Jerusalem (1 Mac. 1:11-15).

[14] This is the common allusion to Deut 6:4, the primary tenant of the Jewish faith, the credo of monotheism.

[15] This refusal is found elsewhere (1 Macc. 2:63)

[16] See Gen. 3:24

[17] The chronology of events appears confabulated, and is likely the result of a scribal error in the transcription of this txt across the centuries.

[18] The meaning of this direction to the audience is unclear. Perhaps there was originally an illumination attached to a source text that is now lost. These were found in Ethiopia as early as the 5th century, around the potential date of the composition of this text.

[19] Likely a transliteration of the Hebrew name 'Abijah', which was a common contemporary name of the 2nd Temple period.

[20] Likely a transliteration of the Hebrew name 'Shelah'

[21] The same as the aforementioned youth who strangled panthers, an attempt to transliterate the Greek noun for panther.

3:2 [The brothers] went with [the king's men] and received martyrdom at that place.

3:3 Now, they begged and praised, and bowed down to the Lord. Their death did not frighten them, nor did the king's punishment.

3:4 [The soldiers] went to the youths, who were led as innocent lambs. Still they were not frightened. When they had reached them, [the king's soldiers] beat, bound, and whipped them. [The youths] were then delivered to the king and stood before him.

3:5 And the king answered them saying, "Why do you persistent men not make sacrifices or bow before my gods?"

3:6 Those brothers, Seela, Abya and Pantos, who were innocent, who had been honored and chosen, and who shone like a jewel of great price, answered him in unison.

3:7 They said to the king, "As for us, we will not bow, nor make sacrifices to heathen idols that have no mind or will of their own."

3:8 They again warned him, "We will never bow for idols of silver and gold, which have been worked by human hands from stone and wood. They have no mind, no spirit and no will. They cannot offer help to their friends, nor harm their enemies."

3:9 To this the king answered, saying "Why do you say these things? They know when you insult them and injure their character. Therefore, why do you affront the great gods?

3:10 The [youths] answered him saying, "They are nothing to us. We shall insult them and will never offer them praise."

3:11 And the king said to them, "I will punish you for the extent of your wickedness. I will extinguish your beauty with flogging, suffering and fire.

3:12 Now, speak and say whether you will or will not give sacrifice to my gods, if you do not oblige, know my punishment will be the whip and the sword."

3:13 They answered him saying, "As for us, we will not make sacrifices, nor bow before heathen idols". [Hearing this] the king commanded that they might be beaten with a large rod and be flogged. After this they were to be torn in two, so that their organs would be made visible[22].

3:14 And so, hearing this, they bound them, imprisoned them, and while they discussed the means that would kill [the youths].

3:15 Without kindness, they took them and locked them in a prison cell, where they stayed three day and three nights[23].

3:16 On the third day, the king ordered that an edict be issued, and that all royal counselors, noblemen, elders and official be gathered together.

3:17 The king, Tseerutsaydan, sat on his throne and commanded that those great youths, Seela, Abya and Pantos, be brought before him, injured and chained.

3:18 They king spoke to them, saying "When you sat these three days, are you ready to

---

[22] This is an unusually means of execution and is incongruent with any historical punishment of the period. It is likely drawn from the martyrdom of the prophet Isaiah, who is said to have been sawn in two by King Manasseh of Judah.
[23] See Gen. 42:17

return here or will you persist in your past evil?"

3:19 Those honored warriors of the Lord, answered him, saying "For our part, we who were cruelly punished will not agree to worship these idols, so filled with sin and all evil, which you praise."

3:20 And that sinner, [the king], was disturbed and commanded that they might be taken to a high place and have their wounds deepened.

3:21 [The king] again order they might be burnt [alive] with the fire of torches to char their flesh[24]. His servants went and did as [the king] had commanded. Yet, those elect men, said to him, "You who have forgotten the law of the Lord, speak [to us]. Our recompense shall overflow beyond measure, whereas your will punishment will be manifold."[25]

3:22 [The king] then ordered that they might set bears upon them, tiger and lions, and all evil beasts in their presence, so these beasts might consume their flesh and bones.

3:23 He commanded the keeper of the beasts, to set them upon [the youths], which he did as commanded. Moreover, [the servants] chained the feet of the great martyrs with tent-stakes, and beat them again, cruelly.

3:24 They were thrown to the wild beasts, who roared, but when [the creatures] appeared before

the martyrs, they hailed them, bowing before them[26].

3:25 They then returned towards their keeper, roaring and frightening him. [The beasts] were then taken to the king's court and were shown to him.

3:26 Yet, these [beasts] killed seventy-five men from the army of the transgressor.

3:27 Many of the people were struck with terror. They were tormented by their fear [of the creatures], until the king abandoned his throne and fled. Then they seized the beasts with great difficulty and moved them to their cages.

3:28 Two brothers[27] of Seela, Abya and Pantos, came and released them from their imprisonment and chain, and said to them, "Come let us escape these apostates and sinner, before they find us."

3:29 But those martyrs said unto their brothers, "It is not right that we might escape after we have offered our testimony. As it is you who are frightened by this, go and make way."

3:30 Those younger brothers said, "We shall stand with you before the king, and if you are condemned, we shall be condemned with you."

3:31 After this, the king went out onto the palace balcony, seeing that the three elect men had been released, and that the five brothers stood together. Those state officials who had punished the brothers, questioned them, discovering

---

[24] This is an extreme measure of execution in the ancient world, intending to maximize the amount of suffering of the condemned. It was reserved for those who committed serious crimes against the established state or cultural order. This is also found in the Book of Jubilees as it relates to the case of Tamar, wife of Judah. Also, See Lev. 21:9.

[25] See Dan. 12:2

[26] This is a common motif in Christian hagiography. Early texts on the lives of saints within the Roman Empire often have this attributed to them, such as the life of St. Sebastiana, St. Janaruius, St. Thecla and the Apostle Paul.

[27] This is an odd introjection into the text, as the two brothers are not previously mentioned.

that they were all brothers and informed the king. The king was disturbed at this and shouted like a wild boar.

3:32 [Thereafter], the king was given counsel, with the intent of pushing the five brothers. He ordered them to be captured and thrown into prison. In their cruelty, they went and put them in prison, placing them in chains and [beating them] with whipping rods.

3:33 The king, Tseerusaydan, spoke saying "These men have blundered and offended my [royal] person. Why should they dare to do so? The evil of their hands is truly great, and if I tell them to come again to me, they will make their designs even more destructive.

3:34 [Therefore], I will let my wrath fall upon them, each to measure the evil of their labor. I will scorch their flesh with flames and reduce them to cinders. I will fling the cinders of their flesh like ashes upon the mountains."

3:35 Saying this, he waited three days, and then gave the order that [his armies] might go and capture those great men. When those men approached [the king], it was ordered that they should be burnt from a large pyre. To add to this cruelty, [the king ordered] that the fire should contain a boiling cask containing sapindus[28], spume[29], resin[30], and brimstone.

3:36 Straightway it was done, and as the pyre burned the [king's] messengers spoke, saying "We have done as you have commanded us. We have sent those men to be subdued."

3:37 [The king] then ordered that [the brothers] cast themselves into the heat of the pyre. The youths, thereafter, did as the king ordered them. Those great men stepped into the flames and gave their souls to the Lord.

3:38 Those who saw this take place observed angels receiving the souls [of the brothers], escorting them to the gardens of Abraham, Isaac and Jacob, in the place of eternal peace and contentment.

Chapter IV:
The Fate of the Bodies of the Brothers

4:1 When that great transgressor heard of their death, he ordered that their flesh be charred in the flames until they were reduced to ashes, to be scattered into the wind. Yet, the great flames were unable to consume the bodies, or even their hair, and they were cast aside from the pyre.

4:2 The fire was cast upon them again, roaring from morning until twilight, but it still did not burn their [bodies]. [Thereafter, the king] said.

---

[28] A common ingredient in folk medicine, here given an ironic purpose.
[29] Salt water or ocean form
[30] The ancient world offers very few plant resins in common usage, most notably frankincense and myrrh, both common products of Ethiopia and southern Arabia, but highly valuable commodities elsewhere. Its use was also commonly reserved exclusively for religious rituals.

"Come and throw their bodies into the ocean."[31]

4:3 [The king's soldiers] went and did as he had ordered, throwing the corpses into the sea. Yet, even when they were thrown into the open ocean, with heavy stones, cast iron and millstones (wherein a donkey turned to grind), they would not sink into the sea. The Spirit of the Lord came upon them and lodged in them, and they floated upon the waves without sinking. Despite the cruelty that [the king] had shown to them, he failed to destroy their [bodies].

4:4 The king said, "Their deaths have caused more trouble for me than their lives. Throw their bodies to the wild beasts, that they might be consumed. If not, what will I do?

4:5 And the [bodies of] the youths were as the king said. Wild beasts and vultures would not come near their corpses. The birds of the air and scavengers obscured the burning sun from them with their wings. Thereafter, the bodies of the five martyrs remained [in that place] for fourteen days.

4:6 During this, those that saw their bodies said that they shone like the mid-day sun for angels had enclosed their bodies like lanterns hidden in a tent.

4:7 For this, the king took counsel, having misgivings about his actions. He thereafter had graves dug to bury the bodies of the five martyrs.

4:8 Now, that same king, who had forgotten the law of the Lord, was reclining in bed one night when the five martyrs appeared before him in the evening. He was disturbed and quickly grabbed his sword.

4:9 It appeared to him that they entered his house at night as thieves, for he was awoken from his dream and stood in fear. He thought that he might escape from his bed down the hall, for he believed that they might kill him or rob him, and he knew only fear causing his knees to quake.

4:10 Therefore, he spoke to them saying, "My lords, what do you desire of me? What do you wish that I should do?

4:11 They answered him saying "Are we not the ones whom you burnt in the inferno? Did you not order that they might throw us into the sea? The Lord has protected our bodies because we had faith in Him, and for which reason you have failed to annihilate us. Those who trust in Him will not perish. Glory and praise be to the Lord! For those that believe in Him are not dissuaded by earthly suffering."

4:12 "Since I did not know that such a penalty would return to me, what should I offer to you as recompense for the evil that I have committed against your person?

4:13 Please, state the gift I must grant to appease you, so that you will not have death consume my flesh, so that my

---

[31] Here the ancient author(s) are again attempting to exhibit both the lack of morality of the king, but also the absence of charity that is commonly given for ancient burial customs. Properly burying a dead alien is regarded as a work of charity (Tob. 1:17-18). Moreover, the act of cremation would have been an outrage in contrast to common Jewish burial customs.

body may not be lowered into Sheol[32] while I live.

4:14 I have sinned against you, please forgive my transgression, for it is in the righteous of the law of your father, the Lord", [the king] said to them.

4:15 The blessed martyrs spoke to him, saying "In the past, you brought evil upon us, we will not repay you with the same evil. It is for the Lord to bring challenges upon every soul, and it is to the Lord whom you must recompense with.

4:16 Yet, it was for your benefit that it was revealed that we live, for the days of your life are short and your ears are still deaf to reason. It may seem that you have killed us, but you have procured our great welfare.

4:17 The priests of your false gods and you will both descend into Gehenna, where there is no escape.

4:18 Woe unto the idols, to whom you bow, having forgotten to bow before the Lord! He who created you, still you disdain [Him] like the spit [of your mouth] and worship those [idols]. You ignore the Lord who fashioned you, bringing you from death into life. Are you not like smoke, here for the moment and tomorrow become nothing?"

4:19 The king answered them saying, "What do you ask of me, so that I may do as you command?"

4:20 "You must save yourself, for fear that you might enter into the fires of Gehenna. It is not for you to save us, who instruct you.

4:21 Your idols fashioned from silver and gold, stone and wood, have no thoughts or knowledge of your soul. They are the work of men's hands.

4:22 Since they do not kill, they cannot save. They do not offer aide to their friends, nor do they show retribution to their enemies. They do not enrich. They do not show righteousness. They cannot make wealth, nor do they create poverty. They deceive you by the authority of those demons who do not wish for you to be spared from death. They will neither help harvest, nor sow.

4:23 Those [demons] do not wish for people to be spared from death; especially those dark-hearted people who believe in [the idols] whom they have fashioned for themselves.

4:24 As the authority of Satan and his demons dwell within them, they will take possession of your heart, that you might drown in the sea of Gehenna.

4:25 You should abandon this pursuit, granting this as our reward, as it was for this purpose that we died. It must benefit our souls to worship the Lord, our creator" they said to him.

4:26 However, he was troubled and frightened, as the five were seen drawing their swords. He shook in terror and prostrated himself before them.

4:27 "Now I know that those dead, who have become dust, will truly rise again, but for my

---

[32] This use of the Hebrew term is curious, as it is a common term in Hebrew and used in Jewish literature, but not frequently noted in Christian compositions. This is perhaps representative of Falasha theological influence in the region.

sake, only a little remains before my own death."

4:28 After which the disappeared from before the king. That same Tseerutsaydan, the conceited, resolved to stop burning their bodies henceforth.

4:29 He took great delight in his idols and in the errors of his mind, which had deceived him for many years. Many were misled as he was, until the time that they recanted and began worshipping the Lord, who created them. However, it was not only [the king] that had sinned.

4:30 There were those who would make sacrifices of their sons and daughters for the demons. As [the demons] work to seduce them in their thoughts and mind, just as they had been educated by Satan, their father, who encourages such doubt against the love of God.

4:31 They marry their mothers and mishandle their aunts and sisters. They abuse their own flesh as they commit this disgraceful task. Since Satan has taken hold of the minds of these people, they say "We will not return".

4:32 [Just the same], that Tseerutsaydan, who did not know God, was conceited, and would vaunt about his many idols.

4:33 If they are to say, "How can the Lord grant sovereignty to those who do not know him, either through is law or through worship?" They will therefore turn to Him in

penitence, for this is how He wishes to test them.

4:34 If they then offer complete repentance, He will show His great love to them and He will maintain that kingdom. However, if they are stubborn, the flame will punish them forever in the fires of Gehenna.

4:35 It is right for a king to fear his God, the Lord, who is sovereign as he is. Moreover, it is right for a judge to be governed by his God, as he passes right judgments under his authority.

4:36 It is for the senators, princes, envoys and dukes to be commanded by their God, just as they are by their rightful sovereign[33].

4:37 For He is Lord over the heavens and the earth, and He composed all of creation. There is no other god above or below who can grant you wealth. It is He who makes [men] rise and fall.

Chapter V:
Recounting Prior Prideful Kings

5:1 One of the sixty warriors[34] was full of pride. The Lord made him swell-up with a spoon of brimstone. He died from this illness.

5:2 Moreover, Hiram built a bed of cast iron and grew proud of his technical skill. The Lord made him disappear in death[35].

---

[33] This notion of legitimate governance is taken from Neo-platonic thought, where the political and ecclesiastical maxim commonly evoked was "as above, so below".
[34] See Son. 3:7

[35] The meaning of this is obscure. This is perhaps in allusion to Hiram, King of Tyre, who is said to have had great technical knowledge which he shared with the Israelite kings, David and Solomon. However, this story does not appear anywhere in

5:3 [Then there was] the proud Nebuchadnezzar, who said "There is no other sovereign without my sovereignty, for I am the god who makes the sun rise in the east." Thus, conceit grew in abundance within him.

5:4 The Lord, therefore, separated him from his people and made him wander the wilderness for seven years[36]. He then made his fortune in the birds of the air and the wild beasts of the desert, until the time that he knew the Lord was his creator.

5:5 When his time came, he knew and worshipped [the Lord] and again returned to his kingdom. Who is there upon the earth who sits in pride against the Lord, his creator?

5:6 Who is there who has violated His law and moral order that is not swallowed up by the earth?

5:7 And you, Tseerutsaydan, have shown pride in the face of your creator. You have done so that he might annihilate you like these men and lower you into the grave for your conceit.

5:8 These men are among those that have entered into Sheol, where there is mourning and grinding of teeth[37]. This is the place where the darkness abides, and where He lowers them into the final abyss of Gehenna, where there is no escape.

5:9 As for you, you are such a man, who will die and be forgotten tomorrow, just as all the prideful kings before you, who must all eventually leave this world.

5:10 For our part, we shall say 'You are like ruined cities, but you are not the Lord, for it is He who created the heavens and the earth and gave you life.'

5:11 He humbles the arrogant and raises up those who were humble[38]. He gives strength to the weary.

5:12 It is [the Lord] that takes life and raises those from the earth, who have died and been buried.

5:13 He releases captives from the tyranny of sin.

5:14 Oh, Tseerutsaydan, king, why do you vaunt about your heathen idols, who offer nothing?

5:15 Since the Lord created the heavens and the earth, the mighty oceans, the moon and the stars. He has prepared a time for everything[39].

5:16 Men toil in their fields, ploughing it until twilight, yet the stars of heaven dwell forever by his command.

5:17 He calls all to the heavens, for it is known that there is nothing that takes place without the Lord.

5:18 He commands the angels of heaven, whom serve him, praising and glorifying His name. The angels surround all those who are to receive life.

5:19 Raphael, the servant of [the Lord], was sent to Tobit[40], saving him in the land of Raguel[41].

---

the biblical narrative, nor is it noted in Josephus. Sine it does not serve any purpose as a fabrication it is likely a small piece of now forgotten regional folklore regarding the 10th century BC monarch.

[36] This account is not noted in the biblical narrative, but is found in the works of Flavius Josephus composed in the late 1st century.

[37] See Lu. 13:28
[38] See Matt. 23:12; Lu. 14:11
[39] See Ecc. 3:1
[40] See Tob. 5:10
[41] See 1 En. 23, also rendered as Reuel and Akrasiel, He is said to be an archangel of earthly justice.

5:20 The holy [archangel] Michael was sent to Gideon[42], to distract him with sumptuous food, so that he might crush the Philistines. He was also sent to Moses, when he helped the Israelites transverse the Eritrean Sea[43].

5:21 For the Lord has said that he leads them, there are no false gods among them.

5:22 [The Lord] sent them into the harvestable fields of the earth,

5:23 And he fed them a harvest of grain, for He loved his people [Israel], showing his affection by giving them gifts of strong honey[44].

5:24 Therefore, you should heed his commands, and follow the will of the Lord, your creator. For He has given you the diadem and granted your sovereignty over the four kingdoms[45].

5:25 [The Lord] has crowned you making you above all people. He has given you the crown that you might love the Lord.

5:26 It is His will that you might love your creator, just as the Lord has loved you. For he has trusted you with the fate of all nations that you might do the will of the Lord and that your reign might flourish upon the earth, and He may abide with you.

5:27 Therefore, do the will of the Lord, that he might protect and act as a guardian for you

against your enemies, that he might rest you upon your throne and shield you under the wings of his care.

5:28 However, you do not understand that the Lord has elected the crown for you to reign over Israel, just as he selected Saul among the children of Israel when he was tending to his father's donkeys[46]. He had him crowned from among his kin and sat him upon the throne of Israel[47].

5:29 [The Lord] gave him a great fortune, dispersed from his subjects. The Lord too has crowned you to rule over His people but behold you must forever look and protect [them].

5:30 The Lord has appointed you over all of them, for you to do his will, that you give life and take it, that you might distinguish between good and evil." [Nebuchadnezzar] said to him.

5:31 "Now the Lord has appointed you over the nations to do his will, whether it be through the lash or through pardon. You must distinguish good from evil, from those who do good, from those who work evil.

5:32 You are a servant of the Lord, who rules in the heavens, and you must do the will of the Lord, who will keep the

---

[42] See Jud. 6:11-23, although the biblical narrative does not mention the name of the angel.
[43] Perhaps better known in the west as the 'Red Sea'. See Ex. 14:1-30
[44] See Ex.16:31
[45] See Dan. 2:27-29, 7:23-24. This allusion to the Book of Daniel draws upon the various metals used by prior world empires: the Babylonians, Medians, Persians and Seleucid Greeks. Moreover, this particular passage has been associated with a symbolic metaphor for the destruction wrought by the reign of Antiochus IV.

[46] See 1 Sam. 9:3
[47] The meaning of this statement is unknown, as Antiochus IV never claimed the title of the Israelite king, only holding political suzerainty over the former geographical region. While this might be intended as a broader general statement on the nature of political authority it may also be interpreted as a rebuke of the authority assumed by the subsequent Hashomeon dynasty. However, for this to be accurate, at least a fragment of this text would have to date to a pre-Christian period.

5:33 There is no one who holds authority over Him, as He is king over all people.

5:34 There is no one who has appointed Him, as He has appointed everyone.

5:35 There is no one who has the authority to remove Him, but He has the authority to remove anyone.

5:36 There is no one who can reprimand Him, for He delivers rebukes to all.

5:37 There is no one who can make Him assiduous, but He requires this for all. The sovereignty of heaven and earth are for Him alone, and there is no one who is beyond His jurisdiction. Everything is revealed through Him, and there is nothing that can be hidden from His continence.

5:38 He sees all that is, but there is no one who has seen him. He hears the prayers of those who say to him 'save me', for He created man in His image[48], and He has heard his supplications.

5:39 Since He is the king who lives from age unto the infinite age, he nourishes creation with His everlasting nature.

Chapter VI:
The Fate of Kings

6:1 Since He crowns the true kings who do his will, the kings have written forthright about [the Lord].

6:2 Because they have done the will of the Lord, He shall have an unseen star[49] appear in the House of Abraham, Isaac and Jacob, David, Solomon and Hezekiah. It shall be there in the garden where all those blessed kings dwell in the house of light[50].

6:3 Heaven's palatial corridors will shine, yet the great halls of the earth are nothing to compare with those in the heavens. Its floor, which is covered in silver and in gold, exhibiting jewels, are pristine.

6:4 How it looks in its infinite luster cannot be seen or thought by any man[51], as the corridors of heaven gleam like jewels.

6:5 Just as the Lord knows the secrets of nature, the corridors of heaven that He created are unknown to any man, as they are hidden by their own radiance. Its floor, composed of silver and gold, jewels, white and blue silk, are unsoiled.

6:6 They are complete in their beatific fullness.

6:7 The holy ones who are steadfast in their faith and virtue, shall inherit the pardon and the love of the Lord.

6:8 And there are waters of redemption that flow from [the garden] and they shine as the sun. There is a house of light within it, and it is surrounded by an elegant perfume.

6:9 The garden holds fruits that are beautiful and cherished, whose look and taste are dissimilar all around that house. There too are vines of olive and grapes, all splendid, with the fragrance of sweet fruit.

6:10 If a man of flesh and blood would enter it, his soul would

---

[48] See Gen. 1:26
[49] See Num. 24:17

[50] See 1 En. 14:15
[51] See 1 Corn. 2:9

depart from his body from the perfect joy that is found there arising from its savory smell.

6:11 Great kings who did the will of the Lord will be beautified there. Their honor and their place are known in the Kingdom of Heaven, where they abide forever and where salvation is found.

6:12 He has shown that their reign upon the earth was celebrated and righteous, therefore their reign in heaven shall be likewise. They shall be honored and exalted in heaven, just as they were in this world. If they do good deeds in this life, they will rejoice.

6:13 However, those kings who did evil during their reigns in the lands that that Lord had given them, they shall be judged for what they owe. They will be judged if they have ignored the destitute, the cries of the poor, rejected the alien[52] and mistreated the orphan[53].

6:14 They did not protect the poor and impoverished from the hand of the rich who rob them. They did not give food and feed the hungry. They did not give drink to those who thirst[54], and they did not listen to the cries of the poor.

6:15 [The Lord] shall take them down into Gehenna, to their dark end, upon the terrible day that the Lord comes. At that time, His wrath shall be cast against them, just as David spoke in his praise, 'Lord, do not punish me in your

judgment and do not admonish me in your chastisement'[55]. Their pains and their eternal fall will continue in accord with the measure of their infamy.

6:16 Princes and kings reign over this world and do not keep my commandment;

6:17 But the Lord, ruler of the universe, is in heaven. The fate of all souls is under his authority. It is [the Lord] who grants favor to those who glorify Him. For He is king over all things, and His love extends to those open to Him.

6:18 As He is Lord of heaven and earth, he knows the beating of your heart[56] and the thoughts of your mind. Any man who pleads with Him with a pure heart shall have his prayer granted.

6:19 He will destroy the great ones in their arrogance, who commit evil against orphans and widows.

6:20 It is not by your power that you inherited your kingdom, and it is not through your efforts that you sit upon your throne. [The Lord] loves to test you," therefore He has made it possible for you to reign, just as Saul did, who ruled over his subjects in his own time. [The Lord] tests you just as He did Saul, who ignored the words of the prophet Samuel and the Lord, and neither employed his army, nor the army of the Amalekite king[57]. Again, it is

---

[52] See Lev. 19:25
[53] See Ps. 10:18
[54] See Matt. 25:35
[55] This allusion is unclear. It may refer to the episode found in 2 Sam. 24:17, but it does not match it well.

[56] Literally the abdominal cavity, here rendered as 'kidney' (ኩላሊት). This line presumes a Galenic understanding of the practice of medicine.
[57] See 1 Sam. 15:1-35

not by your hand that you attained your kingdom.

6:21 The Lord spoke to the prophet Samuel, "Go, and tell them that I am troubled with the violation of the law, for they have worshipped and bowed before idols; they have temples[58] and commit abominations. Tell this to Saul. Go into the nation of the Amalekites and decimate everything, their armies and their kings, starting with each man and ending with their cattle".

6:22 For this reason, He sent Saul to annihilate them, for they affronted the Lord.

6:23 Yet, [Saul] saved the life of their king, and spared their livestock, their beautiful daughters and noble youths from death. Since [Saul] has contempt for my word and ignored my command, go and divide his kingdom", the Lord spoke.

6:24 "In his place anoint the son of Jesse, David, that he might reign over Israel[59].

6:25 Place upon him a suspending demon, who will inhibit and trouble him[60].

6:26 Since I have given him the kingdom, that he might do My will, and because he has refused, I will remove him from the kingdom that was rightly his. Go to him and say 'Should you ignore the Lord, who has crowned you over the people of Israel? Who placed you upon your royal throne?'

6:27 Say to him, 'You have forgotten the Lord, who

granted you your honor and majesty", He said to [Samuel].

6:28 And the prophet Samuel went to King Saul, coming to him while he sat at his dinner table, and when Agag, King of the Amalekites was seated at his left hand[61].

6:29 'Why have you completely ignored the Lord, who has commanded that you are to annihilate the livestock and the people [of the Amalekites]?' [Samuel] said to him.

6:30 Hearing this, the king grew frightened for his throne and told Samuel, 'Come closer to us' and seized his cloak, for Samuel refused to come closer and his cloak was torn[62].

6:31 And Samuel told Saul, "the Lord has divided your kingdom"[63].

6:32 Saul spoke to Samuel publicly, saying "Help me offer atonement for my sins before the Lord that he might grant me pardon'. Samuel refused to speak with him, for he feared the Lord who created him.

6:33 However, [Samuel] did not fear the king who died. For this reason, he stabbed Agag, King of the Amalekites, before he could swallow his food[64].

6:34 A demon had captured Saul, who worked to destroy the law of the Lord. Since he was the Kings of Kings[65], ruler of the universe, the Lord struck down the head of the sinful king because he had no shame.

6:35 For He is Lord of all of the earth, who can dethrone all the princes' and kings' sovereignty, if they do not fear

---

58 Literally transcribed this word would more accurately be transcribed as 'mosques'. (መስጊድ)
59 See 1 Sam. 16:13
60 See 1 Sam. 16:14
61 This is not noted in the biblical narrative.
62 See 1 Sam. 15:27
63 See 1 Sam. 15:28
64 See 1 Sam. 15:32
65 See 1 Tim. 6:15; Rev. 17:14, 19:16

Him. There are none above Him.

6:36 He has spoken saying "the House of David shall rise to fame and prestige, but the House of Saul shall fall. [The Lord] has taken the kingdom from Saul and his children[66]."

6:37 He did this because it offended Him, and because He destroys sinners who offend Him with their evil deeds. The Lord smote the House of Saul and his children, for any man who does not take vengeance upon the enemy of the Lord is the enemy of the Lord.

6:38 When a man who has authority to take vengeance and smite a sinner does not obey the law of the Lord, and does not offer reprisal, he too is the enemy of the Lord. [It is for this reason] that the House of Saul and his children were destroyed.

Chapter VII:
Reward and Punishment under the Law

7:1 Whether you are a prince or monarch, what importance do you have?

7:2 Is it not the Lord who brought you from nothingness into life that you might do His will, abiding under His law and fearing His great judgement? Just as your servants might displease you, who rule over them, the Lord, your governor, might become displeased with you.

7:3 Just as you admonish the sinner without kindness, the Lord shall do the same, striking at you and lowering you into the depths of Gehenna, where there is no exit for eternity.

7:4 Just as you show the lash to those ungovernable, who have no regard for you, what will happen if you have no regard for the Lord?

7:5 He has created you that you might love and fear Him. He has crowned you over all the world, that you might educate His people to the truth. Why would you not fear the Lord, your Creator?

7:6 You must discern between what is right and true, as the Lord has appointed you. [If you do not], do not look to His face for favor in small or large things. Uphold His worship and obey the nine commands[67].

7:7 Just as Moses ordered the children of Israel, saying "I gave water[68] and fire[69] to you, place your hand into what you love." [Therefore], neither go to the right or to the left[70].

7:8 Listen to His word, that I might hear it and do His command. For you might say, "It is beyond the sea, or the ocean or the river. Who will bring His word to me that I might gaze upon it and do as He has said."

7:9 And you may say, "Who will ascend to the heavens and bring down the word of the Lord to me, that I might hear it and obey." The word of the Lord approaches. Behold! For it requires you to confess it

---

[66] See 1 Sam. 28:17
[67] See 1 Tim. 4:13-16
[68] See Ex. 17:2

[69] See Ex. 32:20
[70] See Pro. 4:27

with your tongue and offer charity by your hand.

7:10 You have not heard the Lord your God unless you have heard His Book. And you cannot love Him, nor keep His commands, unless you keep His law.

7:11 You might therefore enter Gehenna forever if you do not cherish His commands. Unless you do the will of the Lord, who grants you honor and notoriety among your people, you are subject to entering Gehenna eternally.

7:12 He has made you above the people, and He has crowned you over the people that you rule. Therefore, be true and just when you think of your Creator, knowing He granted you your kingdom.

7:13 There are those who receive the lash who have offended you, and there are those whom you have pardoned because you remember the Lord and His deeds. There are [also] those whom you cast verdicts upon rightly to correct their judgments.

7:14 Do not show [unjust] favor when looking upon those debating before you. The earth's bounty is your wealth. Therefore, do not accept a bribe to pardon the guilty and punish the innocent.

7:15 If you did His will, the Lord will grant you longevity in this life, but if you offend Him, then He will reduce the length of your reign.

7:16 Know that you will rise again after death, and that you will stand before Him and be examined for all of the deeds you committed, be they good or evil.

7:17 If you do good deeds, you will reside in the garden of the Kingdom of Heaven in the palace where gentle kings abide and are filled with light. For the Lord does not shame the rightful authority. However, if you do evil deeds, you will reside in Sheol-Gehenna, where the unrighteous kings abide.

7:18 The time will come that you will see your infamy, [you will see] the honor of your warriors, your arms hung up; you will see your horses and armies march to the beat of the drums and hear the playing of the harp.

7:19 Yet, when you see this, you think yourselves great and you harden your hearts. You do not think of the Lord who granted your rank. But [the Lord] has said to you, "repent of this, you who has not turned back."

7:20 You have been negligent in the role He has given you. [Therefore], he shall give sovereignty to another.

7:21 Death will suddenly strike you and judgment will be passed at the time of the resurrection. For as all men work, so shall they be judged. [The Lord] shall consider your case and make judgment upon you.

7:22 No one will honor the kings of this world, as [the Lord] is the true judge. On the day of judgment, rich and poor will stand as one. The crowns of the princes of this world shall fall.

7:23 Judgment is prepared for which all souls quake. On that day, the sinners and the

7:24 None shall be hidden. Just as the mother is ready to give birth, and the child in her womb comes into the world for she cannot prevent this, the earth too cannot present this for her inhabitants.

7:25 For the clouds cannot prevent the rains, for the Lord commands them to fall. The Lord's word has created everything, bringing life out of death. The word of the Lord brings all into their grave, and at the resurrection, it does likewise, making the dead rise again.

7:26 Moses spoke, saying "It is from the words that proceed from the mouth of the Lord, and not from grain that a man is sustained."[71] [For this reason], the word of the Lord shall rouse all people from the grave.

7:27 Behold! It is known that the dead shall arise by the word of the Lord.

7:28 Again, the Lord spoke in [the Book of] Deuteronomy, concerning the princes and kings who do his will. "The day has come when they are counted to meet their destruction. I shall take revenge[72] and destroy them on the day of judgment when their feet will stumble[73]" [the Lord] said.

7:29 The Lord spoke to those who know his judgments, "Know that I am your God the Lord, I kill, and I save[74].

7:30 I issue reprimands and I grant pardons. I lower men into Sheol and I send them forth into paradise. There are none who escape my jurisdiction," He spoke to them.

7:31 The Lord spoke of the princes and kings who do not abide by His law, saying "Since the kingdoms of the earth are temporal, passing as the morning does into the evening, they must keep order and my law if they wish to enter the Kingdom of Heaven, if they wish to have eternal life.

7:32 The Lord calls forth the righteous for [His] magnificence and the unrighteous for His judgment. He humbles the sinners and raises up the righteous.

7:33 He will ignore all those who did not do His will and anoint those who acted in union with His will.

Chapter VIII:
The Relationship between the Body and Soul

8:1 Hear me! Let me tell you of the things when the dead shall rise again. They shall build farms and be fruitful. The grapes shall descend from the vines, for the Lord will bring the fruit in its purity, and they will make wine from it.

8:2 What you have planted is small, but it shall grow into branches, into fruit and greeneries.

8:3 The Lord will give it roots to drink the waters of the earth.

8:4 He feeds the sapling with fire and wind. The roots give water to its branches to drink, and the earth gives the sapling its strength;

8:5 but the soul that the Lord created will bear fruit among them all, just as it will among the dead who will arise.

8:6 When the soul is separated from the flesh, He will say "Gather souls up from the four elements- from the earth and

---

[71] See Deut. 8:3
[72] See Rom. 12:19

[73] See Ps. 121:3
[74] See Is. 45:7

the water, the wind and the fire"[75] just as each has done.

8:7 For that which was earth will return to nature as earth, and that which was water will return to nature as water.

8:8 And the winds shall become winds again, and the fire will return again to become hot fire.

8:9 Yet, a soul that the Lord has separated from the flesh shall return to its creator, until He raises it up again and unites it with the flesh at His appointed hour. He will place [the soul] in a garden in his beloved place.

8:10 He will place pious souls in a house of light in the garden, but those souls of sinners He will send away. He will place them in a house of darkness in Sheol, until the appointed hour.

8:11 The Lord said to the prophet Ezekiel, "Call souls from the four corners, that they might be gathered together and become one member[76]."

8:12 When the time comes, He will speak in a single moment saying, "the souls will all gather from the four corners."

8:13 Wind again became wind, and fire will become fire.

8:14 The earth will return to earth, and the wind returns to wind.

8:15 For the Lord will bring a soul from the garden where He had deposited it, and it will be reunited [with the body] in a

word, for its resurrection has come.

8:16 I will again show to you an illustration that sits beside you. When the sun sets, you sleep; and when the day dawns, you arise from your rest, just as you shall after death.

8:17 When you awake it is just like your future rising. For when the night comes all people sleep, as they are shrouded in darkness.

8:18 But at the day's first light, when darkness is banished, and light returned to the world, everyone shall arise and move about the earth, just as the dead shall again [arise].

8:19 In the Kingdom of Heaven, man shall be born again[77] just like this, for the dead shall resurrect just as the living do [at the start of the day], for this world is short lived and the night proceeds.

8:20 As spoke by David, who said "He has made his symbol the sun,"[78] for as the sun shines when it rises, so shall the Kingdom of Heaven.

8:21 Just as the sun shines in the world today, when Christ returns he shall shine, new in the Kingdom of Heaven. For [Christ] said, "I am the sun that does not set, and a torch that cannot be extinguished."[79] The Lord, He is the light [of the world].[80]

8:22 Straightway, [the Lord] shall raise the dead. I[81] shall offer

---

[75] These are the primordial substances of the universe as imagined by Pre-Socratic philosophers in Ancient Greece. The author of this text must have had some exposure to this line of proto-scientific the mindg.

[76] While Ezekiel uses the phrasing "Four corners" regularly (Ez. 7:2, 37:9, 46:22), there is no comparable passage as found here.

[77] See Jn. 3:3

[78] See 2 Sam. 23:4

[79] Presumably this is a reference to Is. 60:20

[80] See Jn. 8:12

[81] This injunction by the author, as he addresses his audience in first person, appears to indicate that this text was composed for didactic purposes originally. We see a similar use of the first person at 8:16 as well, which is fairly unique to this document.

another example of this for you. From the grain you sow, and you save, whether it is a grain of wheat or a kernel of barley, or a kernel of lentil, or any of the seeds man sows upon the earth, none of these will first grow unless it dies and is consumed[82].

8:23 For the flesh of man which we see, when it is consumed and rotten, is fully devoured of both skin and tenacity.

8:24 The earth has consumed it, and it has become like a seventh of the grain. The Lord sends a cloud that showers rain upon His beloved, and the roots grow upon the earth and send forth its leaves.

8:25 After [the seed] has died and is consumed, it can grow and develop its many buds.

8:26 By the will of the Lord, the fruit proceeds from the buds that grow, and He dresses its resolve to grow.

8:27 For just as the seeds that have been sown grow, the silver, leaves, ears and straw are not tallied for you.

8:28 Do not be a fool who does not understand. Look forth and see that the seeds thrive, and likewise, know that the dead shall be told to arise, and they shall rise. [The dead's] restoration is their task.

8:29 Hear this! If you are to sow wheat, it will not grow into barley, nor if you sow barley will it become wheat. I will tell you that it will not grow. How will you gather barley from wheat? How will you gather linseed if you had sown watercress?

8:30 Of all the different types of plants, if you plant figs, will they grow and become nuts? What if you plant almonds, will they grow and become grapes?

8:31 If you plant saccharine fruit, will it grow and become bitter? What if you plant bitter fruit, is it likely to become sweet?

8:32 What about all men? If a sinner dies, how will he arise and be virtuous at the time of the resurrection? What if a virtuous man dies, is it likely that he shall arise as a sinner on doomsday? Every man therefore shall receive tribulation for the work of his hands, and his tribulation will be the result of his sin and handiwork. However, none shall be accused because of the sin of his neighbor.

8:33 A highland tree is planted and sends forth its great branches, but it will become dry unless the heavens send rain for the leaves to become green.

8:34 The cedars will be uprooted from the ground unless the summer rains fall upon it.

8:35 Similarly, the dead will not arise unless the waters of grace[83] fall upon them, as commanded by the Lord.

Chapter IX:
The Sterility of Idolatry

9:1 Into the highlands, the mountains of Gilboa[84], rains will not pardon them, as

---

82 See Jn. 12:24
83 Here the author attempts to draw the clear parallel between the rain waters given by

providence and the water received from the Christian sacrament of baptism.
84 This appears to be an allusion to the death of King Saul, who was killed at Mount Gilboa (1 Sam.

commanded by the Lord. They will not grow grass for the beasts and the quadrupeds.

9:2 The mountains of Elam and the hill country of Gilead will not put up green visage for sheep and goat, nor the antelope and quadrupeds of the wilderness, nor the wild ibexes and hartebeests[85].

9:3 Also, the forgiveness and morning dew, commanded by the Lord, does not give respite to apostates and sinners, who make grave mistakes and monetary crimes. These dead will not rise again. For Demas[86] and Cyprus, who worshipped idols and dug up roots[87], have caused and worked for these things to happen.

9:4 Those who dig up roots[88] and practice sorcery and make war,

9:5 and those who are filled with lust have abandoned the law [of God]. The people of Media and Athens, who worship the idols and who play music to them, singing while they beat drums and play the masinko[89], strumming their harps, will not rise again, unless the waters of forgiveness[90] rest upon them as commanded by the Lord.

9:6 These are among the many who will be convicted on the day dead rise and when the final judgement has come. Those who seek to save their

life[91], and who love the fruit of their labor, still sin from these idols.

9:7 The prodigality of your heart makes you blind. Do you not believe that the dead will live again?

9:8 When the time comes, a trumpet will be blown[92] by the archangel, the Holy Michael, who will make the dead rise again. You will not remain in the grave without arising. Do not doubt this.

9:9 The hills and mountains shall be laid low, and the path will be made clear[93].

9:10 For the resurrection shall come for all those of the flesh.[94]

Chapter X:
Those Who Doubt the Resurrection

10:1 Yet, if it were not true, that people of the past might be buried and rest with their ancestors, beginning with Adam, then Seth and Abel, Shem with Noah, Isaac with Abraham, Joseph with Jacob, Aaron and Moses, for what reason do they wish to be buried in another place?

10:2 Is it for them to rise together with their kin on doomsday? Or at least that their bones will

---

28:4; 31:1-4) following a battle with the Philistines. David curses the mountains, saying "let there be no dew nor rain upon you" (2 Sam. 1:21).
[85] This is a telling list of animals, most of which only appear in East Africa.
[86] It is unclear who this is in reference to. St. Paul makes reference to a person in his travels (Phil. 1:24; Col. 4:14; 2 Tim. 4:10a), who allegedly "loved the world" and deserted Paul in Thessalonica.
[87] This appears to be associated with a pagan practice of divination.
[88] See 1 En. 7:1
[89] An Ethiopian violin

---

[90] Assumedly, this is referencing the Christian sacrament of baptism, but does so through with the parallel to the sterility cursed upon Mount Gilboa.
[91] See Lu. 17:33
[92] See Rev. 8:6
[93] See Is. 40:4
[94] This is a point of Nicene Orthodoxy within Christianity and originally stems from the works of the church fathers Irenaeus and Justin Martyr. It's presence here is overemphasized, perhaps as the intended audience of this text had doubts to the philosophical legitimacy of this type of resurrection to physical immortality.

not be counted among the sinners and pagans, who worship idols? For what reason did they wish to bury them in another place?

10:3 Do not be misled by your own mind when you say, "How will the dead rise after they have died, those who are buried in a grave of ten thousand and whose flesh is rotten?

10:4 At that time, you will look to the grave and say with your limited wisdom, 'A handful of dust will not be found, how will the dead rise again?

10:5 Will you say that the seed you sowed will not grow? Even that seed shall grow.

10:6 Just the same, the souls the Lord has sown shall soon arise. He has created man in His truth, bringing him from death into life. They shall arise in an instant with the word of His salvation. He will not delay raising [them].

10:7 He will again return man to life, away from the grave and death. Why is it not possible for Him to return from death to life?

10:8 Salvation and rising again only proceed because of the Lord.

Chapter XI:
The Fate of Jerusalem

11:1 Harmon[95] was destroyed and her fortress was demolished, as the Lord has brought tribulation upon them for the evil that they committed by their hands. Those men who worship idols in the lands of Edom and Zebulon[96] will be destroyed at that time. When the Lord proceeds forth, who shall accuse those who did not repent in their youth, but did so in their old age? Tyre and Sidon shall weep because of the wickedness of their idols.

11:2 Since they have committed sin, engaging in fornication and the worship of idols, the Lord shall take vengeance and destroy them. Since they did not live in faith of the Lord, their Creator's commands, the daughters of Judah will be vile.

11:3 [Jerusalem] lived in vanity, killing the prophets in her delight. She did not abide in the nine commandments and dutiful worship. When the dead arise, the sins of Jerusalem shall be revealed.

11:4 When that time comes, the Lord will judge her in His great wisdom. He will take revenge and extinguish her for all the sins that she committed prior. She did not repent,

---

[95] This is not a proper noun, but the Hebrew word for fortress/palace that appears frequently in the Hebrew scriptures. Its usage here is of unclear meaning. It is possible that it is associated with the imfamous spot of 'Har Meggido', which had historically been destroyed at several points throughout antiquity by invading armies. Moreover, this identification would fit into the intention of a Christian author, as this is the alleged site of the apocalyptic battle mentioned by St. John the divine (Rev. 16:16), who noted the site as "Armageddon".

[96] The author here might be confusing the alleged boundaries of the tribe of Zebulon with that of Asher, as the tribe of Asher's tribal territorial holdings included part of Galilee and the city of Tyre itself. The emphasis on these Phoenician port cities is mysterious, as they are not frequently associated with the downfall of Jerusalem or with the deceit of Edom. There inclusion is therefore a function of the author's own experience and not of an attempted biblical exegesis.

neither in her splendor, nor in the latter days.

11:5 [Jerusalem] went down into the grave and became like the dust[97]. She did just as her fathers did, residing in their sin. On the day of the resurrection, [the Lord] shall take vengeance and smite those who break the law of the Lord.

11:6 They will have judgment passed upon them, for Moses spoke concerning them, "Their hearts and their minds became like the minds of the [people of] Sodom.

11:7 They are the kin of Gomorrah, and they destroy the law, for their deeds are evil.

11:8 Their law is like snake poison which kills. It is like the venom of vipers which takes life just the same. "

Chapter XII:
Lament for the Many Sins of Jerusalem

12:1 O my child Jerusalem! Your sins are like that of Sodom and Gomorrah! My child Jerusalem, this is the great reckoning that was spoken of by the prophets.

12:2 Your suffering shall be like that of Sodom and Gomorrah's suffering, for they ignored the law, resorting to infidelity and conceit.

12:3 Their infidelity and conceit are untouched by the heavenly waters, which grant humility and forgiveness. Yet in their minds they are fixed on greed which appeals to their own law. They hold no grievances about spilling blood and robbing their fellow man, for they have forgotten the Lord, their Creator.

12:4 Since they do not know their God, the Lord, and will not depart from their wickedness and idols, they are happy with their deeds, and lust upon other men[98] and upon animals[99].

12:5 Their mind's eye has been blinded so they cannot see the truth. Their ears have been deafened, so they cannot hear the will of the Lord who loves them. They do not know the Lord in their deeds. Their minds are just as that of Sodom, and their brethren, Gomorrah, bears wine likewise made from sweet fruit[100].

12:6 Their deeds are as a deadly poison, if they would scrutinize them. Their deeds have been forged as a curse to them, from the day they were committed to the time it merits their destruction.

12:7 As their law abides, their minds have become entangled in the acts of sin, and their bodies have become property of Satan. His fiery deeds are put forward for the procurement of sin. Their laws are products of their minds and never require good deeds.

12:8 When he is humbled and receives baptism[101], by a

---

[97] See. Gen. 3:19
[98] See Lev. 18:22
[99] See Ex. 22:19
[100] See Is. 49:26

[101] While the precise meaning of this passage is obscure, it appears to be referencing the Donatist schism taking place in North Africa starting in the early 4th century. The Donatist faction contended that denier of Christianity could not be re-baptized

12:9 They have lived deeply in the deeds of evil, and [Satan] will make them into devils[102], waiting to eat what has been sacrificed to the idols. This has begun in the House of Israel as she marches to the mountains and the forests.

believer, it is for the sake of the great reckoning. He will make them steadfast in their minds and destroy those repulsive people who are distant from the Lord.

12:10 [Israel] worships the idols forged by her neighbors. Her sons and daughters are given to demons, who do not know how to differentiate between good and evil.

12:11 They spill innocent blood; they spurt and spill the wine of Sodom for their idols.

12:12 They worship Dagon[103], just as he was worshipped by the Philistines. They make sacrifices to him from their flocks and fatted calves. They rejoice in the laziness taught to them by demons to whom they sacrifice. In the spurting and spilling of wine, they wish to do their will.

12:13 [Jerusalem] makes sacrifices to him, relishing the sloth of the demon. They have educated her, blinding her to the Lord, her creator, who nourishes her by day, who loves her and has raised her from the beginning. [He has]

loved her from the very beginning, from her youth, into the bloom of her beauty, and as he grows old until the time of her death.

12:14 "I will pass judgement on the day of the resurrection, for [Jerusalem] did not return to my law. She has not been firm in keeping my commandments, her time in Gehenna shall be until the days of eternity."

12:15 If they were truly gods, let her idols arise again with her, and descend into Gehenna to save her from destruction when the time of tribulation comes. I am unknown to the priests of the idols whom she worships.

12:16 She lives in sin and insults the sacred objects that I keep in the temple[104]. She is wicked for this.

12:17 When they said to her, 'Behold!' These are the Lord's people, Israel. You are the dwelling place of the Lord. The great kings of Jerusalem were reserved for you.' I have made her ruin, for she has grieved My name that I placed in her.

12:18 She boldly proclaims that she is My servant, and that I am her Lord. She teases Me like a conspirator. Yet, she does not hear me, nor does she do my will as if I were her Lord.

12:19 [Those idols] have become a hindrance as they deceive her

---

and return to the church after their betrayal. However, this appears to be a moot point by the author. This is only pertinent as it would not take place in an epoch when the Donatists fought with the orthodox faith.

[102] This is a significant shift in the diction of the text. This term 'devils' (ደያብሎስ), borrowed from Greek, is not used prior, wherein 'satan' (ሰይጣን) was previously used. It is assumed that Chapter XII and the subsequent remaining chapters are from the pen of a separate author.

[103] The employment of the name of this deity is likely a stand-in for the various pagan idols commonly worshipped in Jerusalem in antiquity. There is little evidence to support that it survived into the Roman period. The last recorded reference to temple of Dagon in the Hebrew scriptures is in 1 Mac. 10:83.

[104] This appears to be an allusion to the conversion of the Jerusalem Temple into a pagan shrine under the reign of King Manasseh (2 Ki. 21:4-7).

and distance her from My Person. She is governed by the idols who do not feed or clothe her.

12:20 She offers sacrifices to them and consumes of these sacrifices. She spills blood, slaughters, and drinks wine for them. She burns incense for them to smell, and her idols command her for she permits them to control her.

12:21 [Jerusalem] makes sacrifices of her daughters and sons for them. She offers accolades to them of their affection. She is happy in the things her tongue confesses and at the work of her hands.

12:22 Woe upon her when the day of terrible judgment is cast! Woe unto her idols, whom she admires and is joined with. She shall be thrown with them into Gehenna, underneath Sheol, where the worm does not sleep, and the fire is never quenched.

12:23 Woe to the wickedness of My child, Jerusalem, for you have abandoned your God and worship sundry idols.

12:24 Suffering shall be brought upon you because of your deeds, for you have grieved My Word. Since you were unable to commit yourself to doing what is right, I shall pass terrible judgment for your affectations.

12:25 You have distressed My Word and have not abided by the law that you were bonded by with Me. You undertook to keep My law so that I might support you, I might save you from your opponents, and keep the order that I have charged you with. Therefore, I will ignore

you and will not grant pardon for this great trial.

12:26 You did not uphold this, and I have ignored you. Since I have created you, and you have not upheld My instructions, nor My moral order, I shall judge your guilt on the day of Judgment. For I gave you privilege that you might be My child.

12:27 Yet, just as [the cities] of Sodom and Gomorrah[105] are deprived of My presence, you too shall be deprived of Me.

12:28 I passed judgment and annihilated them. For just as Sodom and Gomorrah were distant from Me, you have abandoned me as well. Still, I was disturbed and destroyed them, for which I am again bothered and will eradicate you since you are of the kin of Sodom and Gomorrah whom I devastated. I will destroy all those whom I have created who distress Me, by looking upon a young wife with lust in their heart, or those who lay with men and animals as they would women. I shall destroy all those who call their name from this world, so they cannot abide in joy and contentment.

12:29 From their infancy until their old age, they had no fear of the Lord upon their faces. They assist [Satan] with all their evil deeds, and for this [the Lord] does not show His displeasure upon them. They do not recant their deeds, as they are full of sin and injustice.

12:30 All the acts of iniquity, theft, arrogance, and gluttony are already set in their minds.

---

[105] See Gen. 19:1-29

12:31 Because of these deeds, the Lord has disregarded them and decimated their nation. He will burn those with [His] flame as they stand in place, until the source of their life is no more. They will pass away from all subsequent ages, for He will not permit one of them to remain.

12:32 Since they have abided in their iniquity, they will stand waiting, destroyed the day of [My] coming, when the terrible judgment shall be cast, those who have offended me with their wicked deeds will not find pardon, not will I grant them forgiveness.

12:33 I have disregarded them, for you will not find pardon since I have become troubled. All of your deeds are of thievery and sin, fornication, gluttony and lies, and all the deeds of iniquity that are offensive to Me. To you, Jerusalem, [My] child, who is full of wickedness, on the day of judgment you will be detained and placed on trial with the others.

12:34 I had made you for your purity, but you corrupted yourself. I had called you My treasure, but you gave yourself to another.

12:35 I had wedded you for purity, but you were given to devils. [For this reason], I will take vengeance and destroy you for your evil deeds.

12:36 Since you did not listen to My word, and because you have not observed My commandments though I loved you, I shall double the heavy vengeance upon you. For I am the Lord, who created you, and I will cast judgment upon all those who are sinners. On the day of judgment, I shall place suffering upon them in proportion to their evil deeds.

12:37 Since you did not observe My word, and have disregarded My judgment, I will find you guilty with the others.

12:38 Woe unto you, Sodom and Gomorrah! Who let no fear of the Lord enter your mind!

12:39 Woe unto your sister, [My] child, Jerusalem, who will be adjudicated together with you in the flames of Gehenna. You will be thrown together into Gehenna, which has been set aside for you. [Therefore], woe to all sinners for their misdeeds!

12:40 Since you did not observe My commandments, nor heed My word, both of you will be cast down into Sheol together on that day of judgment.

12:41 Gentlemen who observe my commandments and My word shall eat from the wealth that was amassed by sinners. For as the Lord as spoken, "The gentle shall be give the treasure stolen by the evil, and as such the gentle shall rejoice.

12:42 And malefactors and sinners will weep, they shall be oppressed by the sins they committed, having deviated from My command.

12:43 Those you keep My word and abide as I command, they shall find benediction and sit in righteousness beside Me.

12:44 Those who keep My word and abide under it will eat from the fat of the land. They will reside in the garden of gentle kings, whose hearts are pure.

31

Chapter XIII:
Punishment for All those Who are Deceptive

13:1 When I go forth to seize them, they shall be despicable and perish from My great wrath. Woe unto Tyre and Sidon, and all the land of Judah who fill themselves with arrogance this day.

13:2 The Lord of Hosts said this, "The children of the devil, full of conceit shall be born of them- the false messiah, the enemy of all truth. They are out of their minds and brashly claim that they do not know God." He added, "Woe unto them! The Lord, the king of the universe, has said 'I made man for the designs of my anger, so that I might be revealed in this.'"

13:3 Capernaum, Samaria, Galilee, Damascus, Syria, Achaia, Cyrus and the lands of the Jordan are all the people who have limited their minds, who live in sin and whom are covered by the dark shadow of death. For devils have hardened their hearts and they are commanded by them, as they do not return in fearing the Lord.

13:4 Woe unto men on that day, who are counseled by demons and offer sacrifices to their name. They have denied the Lord their God. They are like creatures without minds. That false messiah[106] who forgot the law of the Lord is a child of the devil. He will establish his likeness in all places, for he has said 'I am a god.'[107] He will be content in the thoughts of his heart, in the work of his hands and in his thievery and all his sinful acts of treachery and iniquity. He will be known by his fornication and burglary.

13:5 It was known from the beginning to the Lord that this should come to pass, the time is known for all those who are sinful.

13:6 The sun will darken, and the moon will turn to blood,[108] and the stars will be shaken[109] from the heavens. All the actions will cease, and the miracles that the Lord has wrought will be brought forward in the age of fulfillment, so that the earth might pass away. He will make all things pass away, both those who live in sin and those who abide within Him.

13:7 While the Lord has pride in his creation, He made all of His beloved in haste, in one short hours. The angel of death shall destroy one small enemy, the devil.

13:8 The Lord, the ruler of the universe has said, "I shall pass My judgment and destroy", but after the arrival, for the devil has no authority.

13:9 "On that day [the devil] shall be apprehended under my wrath and he thrown down into Gehenna, which has been

---

[106] This appears to be an approximation of the term 'Anti-Christ', as it would have been known through the letters of St. John (1 Jn. 2:8, 22, 4:2-3; 2 Jn. 1:7) as well as through the Gospels (Matt. 24:24; Ma. 13:22)

[107] This conception of the Antichrist claiming divinity is first noted by the african church father Tertullian (On the Resurrection, XXIV) in the early 3rd century. It is reiterated by Hippolytus (Treastise on Christ and Antichrist, II). In all likelihood, this tradition of the antichrist is taken from St. Athanasius, who noted in 'Four Discourses' that Arius was the 'harbinger of Antichrist'.

[108] See Rev. 6:12; Jo. 2:31; Acts 2:20

[109] See Matt. 24:29; Ma. 13:25;Rev. 6:13

prepared for him and where punishment awaits. He will bring with him many into the punishment and destruction, because of his treachery; for I am He who detains and releases all those from Gehenna, where he will be cast."

13:10 He grants strength and resolve to the weak. Again, he grants strength and resolve to the weak. Therefore, let those who are strong not become boastful because of their authority.

13:11 Since he is sovereign, and adjudicates between the guilty and the innocent, He will return the misdeeds committed against widows and orphans.

13:12 "Woe unto those who are boastful and proud of heart, to all those who think I do not rule over you or will not cast judgment upon you or smite you. In their conceited and arrogant talk, they have said 'I will expand your throne into the stars of the heavens. I will be as great as the Lord."

13:13 [The Lord] shall speak, saying "Woe unto you who are as the devils who fell from heaven[110], the one who shone like the morning star[111], that I created before you.

13:14 You have dared to utter this in your arrogance. You have ignored the Lord who formed you by His power. Why have you swaggered, so that you might descend into Gehenna because of the hardness of your heart?

13:15 You were corrupted apart from those angels who were made as you are. They offer praise to their creator with humble hearts, for they knew He forged them from fire and wind. They do not deviate from His commands, and keep their hearts free from treacherous thoughts, so that they abandon His commands.

13:16 Yet, you acted treacherous, emboldened by your arrogance. You became wicked, removed from your companions. You have loved the sin and all iniquities! Theft and sedition belong to those who abandon the law of the Lord, and to sinners like you. Those who are kin to you, those who are transgressors like you, abide by their own desires, as you have taught them to sin.

13:17 Woe unto you! Those demons whom you deceive in your malevolence will be cast with you into Gehenna forever.

13:18 Oh, children of the Lord, who have been misguided by that transgressors, the devil, woe unto you! Since you have been mistaken by his intentions, which he and his armies have taught you, you will be cast into Gehenna forever, where there is no escape.

13:19 Previously, when Moses, the servant of the Lord was among you, you offended the Lord at the place of dispute over the waters[112], and also upon [Mount] Horeb[113], and against

---

[110] See Is. 14:12
[111] The absence of 'Lucifer' as the proper name for satn here suggests that this is an allusion composed before the time of St. Jerome's Vulgate. However, this identification of the text of Isaiah with satan is the interpretation of early church fathers. Certainly,

Origen and Tertullian make with identification with the rebellious angels, as this author must have been at least indirected influenced by the corpus of their theological ponderings.
[112] See Ex. 17:2-7
[113] See Ex. 17:6

the Amalekites[114], and upon Mount Sinai[115].

13:20 In the past, when you had sent scouts into [the land of] Canaan[116], they spoke to you, saying, "The way is distant, and the ramparts of their fortresses reach up to the heavens and are mighty. Great warriors must abide there." From this you were disturbed, and thought to return to the land of Egypt, where you toiled[117]. For this you grieved the word of the Lord.

13:21 You did not think of the Lord, who made you strong in your suffering, who performed astounding feats in Egypt and who guided you under the direction of His angels. By day he would set a veil of clouds around you, so that the sun would not burn you; by night, He would have a column of flames shine so that you might not stumble in the darkness.

13:22 In those days, the army of the Pharaoh had frightened you and you wept to Moses, who wept to the Lord. The Lord, therefore, sent his angels[118] to protect you and prevent you from encountering Pharaoh.

13:23 [The Lord] sent them to the Eritrean Sea in suffering, as He leads only Israel. Thus, He spoke, saying "There are no sundry idols among you." And for this, he drowned all their enemies in the sea at once. He gave refuge to none who fled[119].

13:24 [The Lord] made Israel cross the sea by foot, and they were spared from the punishment prepared for them by the Egyptians. [The Lord] then brought them to Mount Sinai[120], where He fed them manna for forty years.

13:25 Nevertheless, the children of Israel offended the Lord again. He had done this mighty thing for their benefit, yet they abandoned the worship of the Lord.

13:26 They thought evil thoughts, from their youth until old age. The torah[121] written in the land of their father's birth, was directly from the mouth of the Lord. Thus, He has spoken, "The children of Adam will become as dust[122], and all of their deeds are directed to thievery. They embrace evil. There are none among them who will take on honest work. They are only for hoarding wealth, violence, deceit, burglary and iniquity. They welcome evil into their hearts."

13:27 They all accept evil deeds in the days when they abide in life. The children of Israel, who destroyed the law of the Lord have made Him grieve, from ancient days until the age of fulfillment.

---

[114] See Ex. 17:8-16
[115] See Ex. 32:1-24
[116] See Num. 13:1-2
[117] See Num. 13:28-32
[118] See Ps. 78:49
[119] See Ex. 14:25-27
[120] See Ex. 19:1-2

[121] The reference to the torah (orat), as a term for the ancient Hebrew law is conspicuous, as a Christian author/audience would have little use for this allusion. Perhaps then the audience was intended to be Falasha, or those already familiar with the historic tenants of Judaism.
[122] See Gen. 3:19

Chapter XIV:
The Moral Order of God

14:1 In the days when the Lord destroyed the children of Cain, their companions were destroyed before them in the great flood because of their sins. [The Lord] baptized the Earth in the waters of decimation. He purified the earth from all of the sins committed by the children of Cain.

14:2 [The Lord] has said, "I regret making mankind."[123] He eviscerated all transgressors and did not spare any, but eight people. He annihilated everything. After which, He had them multiply and they filled the earth[124]. They partook in the inheritance of Adam, their father.

14:3 Noah swore an oath to the Lord. They all made an oath with Him, so that the Lord may not again send a flood to destroy the earth. The children of Noah may consume meat, but not while it has life within it[125]. They must not worship the many idols, but only the Lord, who created them. As such, [The Lord] would be a loving father to them, and not destroy them again because of their sinful vanity, or send away the early spring rains, or give away their flocks, people or sustenance. He will give them grass and grains, fruits and trees, that they might perform righteous deeds that please the Lord.

14:4 After the Lord gave this command, the children of Israel grieved Him with their sins. They did not abide in his law. As their fathers Isaac, Abraham and Jacob had not sought to destroy the law of the Lord.

14:5 Starting among the humble to the great, the children of Israel abandoned the law of the Lord and were dishonest in their deeds.

14:6 The priests, scribes, and chiefs all destroyed the law of the Lord, regardless of their position.

14:7 They do not abide in the order of the Lord and His laws, which Moses had spoken to them in Deuteronomy "Love your God, the Lord, will all your body and all your heart."[126]

14:8 They do no abide in the order of the Lord and His law, which Moses implored them, "Love your neighbor as yourself. Do not worship his many alien idols. Do not covet a young man's wife. Do not murder. Do not steal.

14:9 Do not bear witness in a falsehood. Do not covet your neighbor's wealth, whether it is his donkey or his ox, or anything owned by your brother."

14:10 When he had spoken all this to them, the children of Israel turned again to their betrayal and sin, holding fast to theft and iniquity, towards lust, falsehood, burglary and idol worship.

14:11 The children of Israel offended the Lord on [Mount] Horeb, by forging a [golden] cow that grazes. They all prostrated themselves, saying, "Behold! These are our gods, who have

---

[123] See Gen. 6:6
[124] See Gen. 1:8

[125] See Gen. 9:2-4
[126] See Deut. 6:5

sent us out of the land of Egypt."[127]

14:12 They thereafter rejoiced at the work of their hands. They feasted and were satisfied, rising only to offer praise.

14:13 The Lord spoke unto [Moses], saying "Your people, whom you brought forth from the land of Egypt, where they were oppressed, have deviated from the law and have done evil. They have forged the image of a calf, and now bow to this idol." Moses was filled with anger from this and departed from Mount Sinai.

14:14 For this the anger of Moses fell upon his people. He spoke with fury with his aide, Joshua, who heard him speak "Behold! I have heard in the camp of Israel the singing of warriors!"

14:15 Moses said to Joshua, "It is the frivolity of Israel, drinking unpure wine. Are they songs of warriors? I think not." In his rage he smashed the idol, breaking it into dust. [Thereafter], he mixed [the dust] with water, so that the children of Israel might drink of it beside the mountain[128].

14:16 Subsequent to this, he ordered the priests to kill the others because of the iniquity they committed in the presence of the Lord[129].

14:17 They knew that this act of defiance against the Lord had merited death, and the death of their fathers. [Therefore], they did as they had been commanded.

14:18 Again, Moses spoke to them, saying "You have offended the Lord, who has sustained you, His beloved, who sent you forth from the house of tyranny. [It was He] who has granted you the inheritance that He promised to our ancestors, due to all their respective children. Yet, because of this deed you have not made the Lord glad.

14:19 For they walked in the ways of sin and evil; they did not stop their offenses against the Lord in that place.

14:20 They are unlike their ancestors, Isaac, Abraham and Jacob, who made the Lord rejoice in the work of their hands, so that they might be given what they possess upon the earth. [The Lord] has prepared heaven for all those who love Him, from their birth to their youth and old age. Yet, they are dissimilar to Abraham, Isaac and Jacob, who made him rejoice with the work of their hands, so that He might grant them the land to inherit where joy and happiness are to be found upon the earth. It is a garden that makes all delight and has been prepared for all those gentle people in the world to come. He has prepared this for Abraham, Isaac, and Jacob who made the Lord rejoice while they lived and showed Him their love, which eye has not seen, nor ear has heard[130], and which cannot be imagined in the mind.

14:21 Their children, who denied the Lord, were evil and abided by their own desires. They do not hear the commands of the Lord who had nourished them, watching over them from their youth.

---

[127] See Ex. 32:1
[128] See Ex. 32:21-24
[129] See Ex. 32:26-28
[130] See 1 Cor. 2:9

14:22 They have no thought of the Lord, who sent them forth from the land of Egypt, who saved them from tyranny and oppressive toil.

14:23 However, they deeply offended Him, and He sent the neighboring peoples upon them. They would grow in animosity and tithe them as they desired.

Chapter XV:
Revolt against Akrandis the King

15:1 At that time, the Midianites rose up against them in animosity. They raised their armies and marched against Israel, that they might make war. Their king was called Akrandis[131], and he quickly marched his great armies from Cilicia, Syria and Damascus.

15:2 They made their camp across the Jordan, and [the king] sent messengers saying, "So that I might take hold of your wealth, send the tithes of Israel to me." He said to them, "If you refuse to pay this tithe, I will come and take vengeance, carrying away your cattle, horses and children

15:3 I will make you captives and take you into an alien land. There you will labor as irrigators and wood gatherers,[132]" he said to them.

15:4 Do not clamor and say, "We are the Lord's people. There is nothing impossible for us." Is it not the Lord who sent me to destroy you and carry off your wealth? Am I not the one whom the Lord sent to gather your people together?

15:5 Is there really salvation in those different idols whom I have destroyed? I have captured all your horses and slain then. I have taken your children hostage.

15:6 "Unless you levy this tax as I command you, I will destroy your people" [the king] said. Therefore, he crossed the river Jordan, spoiling their wealth, abducting their cattle and taking their wives.

15:7 And the children of Israel went weeping and mourning to the Lord. They cried to Him for the required one to save them.

15:8 For this reason the Lord gave strength to the three brothers, whose names were: Yihuda[133],

---

[131] This is the Ge'ez transliteration of the name 'Alexander'. There are three potential identities for this individual, assuming that this story is attempting to recount a historical or semi-historical personality. Firstly, it may be used to identify Alexander the Great as a personification of all Greek culture. However, Alexander as he is mentioned in Catholic/Orthodox texts is given due reverences and not as an enemy of Jewish worship. Moreover, this personification would not advance the moral intent of the author who remains focused on religious orthodoxy and not the political independence of the Jewish people. Secondly, this might reference the Jewish king Alexander Jannaeus, who made enemies internally within Judaism in his assumption of the crown. However, this identification is also improbable given that he is identified as a powerful monarch the greater Levantine region. Thirdly, and perhaps most plausibly is that it references the Seleucid king, Alexander I Balas, who succeeded Antiochius IV and reigned from 150 to 145. However, his use as the antagonist of the Maccabees is confused, as we are told in the familiar account of Maccabees that he appoints Jonathan as High Priest in Jerusalem (1 Mac. 10). However, his death as reported by Polybius and Josephus does appear to be similar to the events recounted here.

[132] This is intended to be particularly demeaning as these are the tasks of unskilled laborers.

[133] This is a Ge'ez transliteration of the common Hebrew name Judah. However, this cannot be identical to Judah Maccabee as the chronology is entirely different from the familiar account of the Maccabee revolt. Who these brothers are is unclear.

Mebikyas[134] and Meqabees, who had beautiful features and were cunning warriors[135].

15:9 The children of Israel wept when they had heard [the edict]. It filled their hearts with woe and caused all the children of Israel to shout. The orphans, widows, the elders and priests, and all of the people of Israel, men and women and all of their children, wept and put ashes upon their heads[136]. Their princes wore sackcloth.

15:10 The brothers, therefore, who were striking and bold, went forth and agreed that they might save [the people]. They took counsel, saying "Let us go and die for the sake of the nation!"

15:11 They then said to each other, "Take the heart of grace! Take the heart of grace! They then went forth gripping their swords at their waist and holding fast to the spear in their hands. They went ready for the battle to come.

15:12 When they had reached their camp, Mebikyas attacked the warrior-king while he was seated at his dinner table. He severed his head with a single blow while his food was still in his mouth[137]. Meqabees and Yihuda fell upon the armies of the king, planking them and killing all among them.

15:13 When their king had been soundly defeated, they pierced their compatriots' hearts with their spears and fled from that place. Their bows[138] were broken, and they had been defeated.

15:14 Those brothers were spared from death, as there was no evil found within them. Despite this, the Lord placed his great judgment upon them, and they lacerated each other until they the time that they were exhausted.

15:15 They defeated themselves, dying after crossing the [river] Jordan, but before they traversed [the river] they cast away all their wealth. When the children of Israel saw that their enemies had retreated, they went into their camp and plundered it. They carried away the wealth for themselves.

15:16 The Lord saved Israel through the brothers and the hand of Mebikyas.

15:17 Israel waited several days to praise the Lord.

15:18 However, they again adopted their same sin. The children of Israel were negligent in their worship of the Lord.

15:19 He shall therefore make them slaves, by sending aliens who will steal their grain, destroy their vineyards, abduct their flocks and slaughter their livestock before them.

15:20 They will seize their wives and children because they have offended the Lord. Since they are people who have destroyed the law, [their enemies] will smash the heads of their children[139]. None will be saved.

---

[134] This name is of disputed meaning. It appears to be a phonemic inversion of the word 'Maccabee'.
[135] Unlike the aforementioned group of brothers, these three are not mentioned in the Ethiopian Synaxarion.
[136] See 2 Sam. 13:19; Num. 19:9; Es. 4:1; 1 Mac. 3:47

[137] This account seems identiifcal to the account of the death of Agag, King of Amalekites, who was previously mentioned at 1 EthMac. 6:33.
[138] 'yemīgetiru'- a common weapon of Axumite and Kushite armies, but not heavily used by Hellenic kings.
[139] See Ps. 137:9

Chapter XVI:
The Many Enemies of Israel

16:1 Those who commit this act are Tyre and Sidon, and all those who reside beyond the river Jordan and upon the crest of the ocean. [They are from] Haran, Gilead, Jebus, Canaan, Gergesa and among the Amalekite peoples[140].

16:2 All people act as this, residing among their own tribes and nations, each section of the earth with separate deeds and tongues, all set to the task that the Lord has given to them.

16:3 There are men who know the Lord, and their acts are good.

16:4 Yet, there are men who do not know the Lord who made them, and their actions are wicked. Those that commit sin shall be governed by the hand of Shalmaneser, King of Syria[141].

16:6 The lands of Gilboa, the people and Persia and Media, Cappadocia and Shewa[142], all those who reside in the western mountains, and in the fortress of Gilead and in Phasthos[143], which lies in the land of Judah, they are many who reside in these regions.

16:7 Their neighbors do not know the Lord, nor do they attempt to keep His commandments, their hearts are hard.

16:8 He shall give them destitution for the evil that they have committed by their hands.

16:9 As for the people of Gilead, Caesarea and that of the Amalekites- they have all become one people, destroying the nation of the Lord, which was filled with the truth and where the God of Israel was praised. The One whom the angels serve as chariots of Cherubim, the most high and sovereign, they serve Him in fear and trembling. He shall repay them in destitution for the evil that they have commited by their hands[144].

Chapter XVII:
Rebuke of the Edomites

17:1 The Amalekites and Edomites do not worship that Lord, from whom the sovereignty of the heavens and the earth is contested. They are sinners who do not live by the truth and are not afraid of demolishing the House of God, the temple[145].

17:2 They have no fear of the Lord above them, for they shed blood, commit buggery, and consume that which has been slain and offered as sacrifice to dead idols. They are fully rebuked transgressor.

---

[140] This is a list of the historic enemies of the the Israelite tribes in antiquity. However, Gergesa only appears in the Greek Scriptures in reference to an ethnic group found only in Galiliee (Ma. 5:1-20; Lu 8:26-39; Mat. 8:28-34)

[141] While there are technically five kings of the Assyrian Empire with this name, the author here appears to be alluding toe Shalmanesar V, who gained notoriety for the destruction of the northern Kingdom of Israel and the destruction of the ten (lost) tribes. This is perhaps a circuitous way of rendering deuteronomistic theology. That is to say, immoral deeds of the individuals of a particular country will have repercussions to the national welfare.

[142] This appears to be the author's estimation for both the far north and the far south.

[143] This Greek loan word is mysterious as it is a rendering of the word 'pheasant', but it corresponds to no known location.

[144] This line is a repetition of the former line, 16:8

[145] See Ps. 137; Lam. 4:21-22

17:3 They have no morals, nor religion. Since they hate virtue and do not know the Lord, they are estranged from charity. They know only robbery and sin, pestiferous and cruel deeds, frippery and song as they were taught by the devil, their father. They have no morals, nor religion.

17:4 He governs them with his demonic army, and instructs them on all the evil deeds that they might commit- robbery and sin, theft and deceit, stealing money eating carcasses and committing buggery.

17:5 [The devil] teaches those who are committed to these acts-abducting a young wife, murder, consuming the meat dedicated to idols, slaying a man in violence, jealousy, gluttony, and all the evil deeds that are beyond the love of God. Those devils are their enemy, they instruct them on this subject that they might grow estranged from the law of the Lord, who is sovereign over the universe.

17:6 The works of the Lord are full of virtue and modesty, not in pestiferous actions to your brother, but to charity for your neighbor, in compassion and love to all men.

17:7 Do not be like hypocrites[146] who are good when seen by others, and do not be like the wicked, nor thieves, nor those who abduct young brides, nor men who do evil to their neighbor, nor whose who wrong their neighbors in violence.

17:8 [Those demons] are coy, shaking their heads to provoke evil. They dishearten and deceive many, who are lowered into eternal punishment.

Chapter XVIII:
The Fate of the Angels and the Sons of Seth

18:1 Know that after death you will see the Lord, in whose hand all people dwell. You will stand before Him and He will examine you for all the transgressions that you committed.

18:2 The children of the elite, those who are full of conceit and evil, will become weak and humbled, for they saw their greatness, but did not put the Lord before them. They were ignorant to the Lord, who created them, granting them life out of non-existence.

18:3 In ages past, when their fathers, who were as the angels, worshiped on the mountaintops with the angels, they were deceived. They thereafter descended[147] into this world where tribulation shall pass into eternity.

18:4 In ancient days the Lord created human flesh for them, granting it to them though they deceive and are arrogant, so that they might be properly tested to keep his command. Yet, [despite this], they took wives from the children of Cain.

18:5 They did not obey His law, and He threw them into the fires of Gehenna[148] with their father, the devil. For the Lord

---

146 See Matt. 6:5
147 See 1 En. 6:1-7

148 See 1 En. 21:6-7

was displeased with the children of Seth who wronged one another, and the length of their lives were shortened because of their transgressions.

18:6 They brought the children of Adam into sin with them, and for this [the Lord] has lowered them all into Sheol where they shall wait for punishment.

18:7 The longevity of people has been shortened because of the blunder of the children of Seth by the children of Cain. In ancient days, a man lived to the age of nine hundred.

18:8 The Lord said, "Since they are composed of flesh and blood, my spirit of life will not abide in them forever."

18:9 And for this reason, our life was cut short because of our great sin. Our life is terse compare to our ancestors, who came before us. For when they were but young children, we are dying.

18:10 The lives of our ancestors prospered for they kept the laws of [the Lord] and they did not seek to offend Him.

18:11 Yet, while their lives were bountiful, they were troubled by their daughters who would not be taught. They were concerned because their sons sought to destroy the law of the Lord.

18:12 That time was truly magnificent because they did not annihilate the law of the

Lord with their sons and daughters.

Chapter XIX:
The Fault of the Children of Seth

19:1 When the children of Cain grew in number, they forged drums, harps, sistrum[149] and violins. They wrote songs and pursued leisure.

19:2 The children of Cain were beautiful, born of the former wife of the gentle Abel, whom [Cain] killed for her. For she too was beautiful, and after he killed his brother, he took her for she was his wealth[150].

19:3 He left his father and went into the land of Cephas[151], which lies towards the west. His children were found to be beautiful as was their mother[152].

19:4 Subsequently, the children of Seth went upon Cain's children. And when they saw them, they did not wait a single moment, they choose from among the women, their wives.

19:5 They took us into their great fault because of this, and the Lord was troubled and disturbed by them.

19:6 The devils teased them saying, Come, you will become like gods, just as your creator the Lord"[153]. He ensnared our

---

[149] The exact rendering of this word is insightful to its authorship. The text calls it 'santee', which appears nowhere else in Ethiopian texts, as it is a cognate from the Greek word 'seiein' mixed with Coptic grammar, meaning "the shaker". The author's formal and ecclesiastical education is likely from Greek scholars within the city of Alexandria.
[150] This detail is not included in either the biblical narrative nor in the Book of Jubilees.

[151] This location is unknown. Nor is it clear why the 'land of Nod' (Gen. 4:16) is replaced with this Aramaic term for 'stone'.
[152] Curiously, the author does not use the proper name for Cain's wife, Awan, found elsewhere in in the Ethiopian Bible (Jub. 4:9).
[153] See Gen. 3:5

mother, Eve, and father, Adam, into his fault.

19:7 In their foolishness, they saw it to be the truth, they removed themselves from the law of the Lord, who had created their being, and whom they had formerly bowed, praised and glorified.

19:8 Yet, the Lord expelled them, Adam and Eve, who thought they could attain divinity of their own accord. He humbled them because of their arrogance.

19:9 Just as David spoke, saying "Adam perished because of that transgressor, the devil's arrogance"[154]. Our father Adam was condemned under the Lord's good judgment because of the devil's arrogance.

19:10 Just the same, the children of Seth were guilty by proxy of the sin of Cain. For this, the Lord has granted us shorter lives than that of our ancestors.

19:11 Yet, there were those who had done good and they were resolved to the Lord, for they instructed their sons and daughters and kept them close to the law of the Lord. They therefore found no evil intent among their enemies.

19:12 For it does not benefit them to do good deeds, if they did not properly instruct their own children.

19:13 Just as was spoken by David, "They did not disguise anything from one child to another. Instruct them to praise the Lord and the great deeds He has done through His majestic strength." For it does not benefit them, if they did not properly instruct their own children and their progeny, so that they might know and do the will of [the Lord]. They might, therefore, teach them to trust in the law of the Lord, just as their ancestors did, who made the Lord pleased with their good works.

19:14 Those ancestors who taught them trust from their youth have kept the commands of the Lord. Like their ancestors, they learned to worship the Lord and obey the nine laws.

19:15 Those children learned from their ancestors to praise their creator, to keep His laws, to do good deeds and to love Him.

19:16 [The Lord] shall hear their prayers. He will not ignore them as He grants forgiveness.

19:17 His wrath has grown, but He will not turn it towards them, for He will not annihilate everyone in his tribulation.

Chapter XX:
Promise made to the Faithful

20:1 My brothers[155], do not forget what you have been told- that the Lord keeps sees the work of those who do moral things.

20:2 He shall multiply their progeny in this world, and their names will live in pious memory for eternity when invoked. Their children will not hunger for bread in this world.

20:3 He shall guard them for their [ancestors'] sake. He will not turn them over to the enemy. He will save them from the designs of their enemy who hates them.

---

[154] There is no biblical parallel attributed to this statement by David.

[155] This introjection by the author appears to be directed to an ecclesiastical audience.

20:4   For all those who adore His name, he shall be an advocate in their time of trouble. He will protect them and forgive them of their sins.

Chapter XXI:
The Welfare of earlier Judahite Kings

21:1   David had faith in the Lord, for the Lord had faith in him. He protected him while he was in flight from the hand of Saul the king.

21:2   [David] had faith in Him and obeyed the law, when his son Absalom arose against him, and when the Philistines arose against him, and when the Edomites and the Amalekites arose against him, and when one of the four at Rephaim[156]. The Lord saved David from all the suffering brought on from the enemies he fought.

21:3   Those who prevail do so by the will of the Lord, and as such, they were struck down by their enemies. The Lord did not spare the wicked kings who had no faith in Him.

21:4   Hezekiah believed in the Lord, who saved him from Sennacherib, the arrogant.

21:5   Yet, his son, Manasseh[157], found defeat at the hands of his enemy, for he did not trust in the Lord. He did not have faith in the Lord and showed no fear to his God who had given him glory and honor. They bound him and took him from his nation. However, the enemies of [King] Manasseh were unlike him.

21:6   Upon that hour, [the Lord] deprived him of the kingdom He had given to him, for he committed no righteous deeds before the Lord God. The years of his life would be great and [the Lord] might ward off his enemies, if he did so, and he might have majesty all around him.

21:7   It is better that you have faith in the Lord, then in countless armies, with their horses, bows and shields.

21:8   Faith in the Lord exceeds all. A man who has faith in Him shall abide in majesty and magnitude.

21:9   The Lord does not indulge your continence. All those who do not believe in [Him], who place their faith in their wealth, will become separated from it and will lose the dignity given to them by [the Lord].

21:10   [The Lord] shall protect all those who believe in Him. He shall make men confabulated who regard Him as confabulated. Since they did not discipline themselves to follow the Lord and His law, He will not spare them from the time of tribulation when they clash with their enemies.

21:11 to   Yet, to all those who hold tight the worship of the Lord and obey his laws, [the Lord] shall be an asylum in times of trouble[158].

21:12   He will destroy his enemy, plunder his enemies cattle, capture the men of his enemies' nation,

21:13   send rain year after year, make their fields green, sending forth the spring rains and storing great piles of grain and

---

[156] See 2 Sam. 5:18-22
[157] See 2 Chr. 33:11-13

[158] See Ps. 91:2

fruit, so that his people might rejoice. He shall make them all rejoice!

21:14 He shall make them rejoice because they will consume the wealth of their enemies! They will be satiated by taking their wealth, despoiling it from their enemies, taking from them their cattle, sheep and cows. They will rightfully devour them at their tables and take the children of their enemies as captives.

21:15 The Lord shall perform this deed for all those whom He loves, but those who despise [God] will feel the lash of their enemy.

21:16 His hands and feet shall be bound, and he will be given into the hands of his enemy. [The Lord] shall offer him up to be mocked by his adversary. For, as he shed blood, and destroyed the law of the Lord, none of his descendants will rejoice.

21:17 He will not find life at the time of judgment, as [the Lord] brings tribulations upon all sinners. He will place further hardship upon the wicked.

21:18 Yet, it has been spoken by the Lord, that those who are righteous will find their reward, and they might abide in the creation of [the Lord].

21:19 For he is sovereign over the whole of creation, and his creatures are to offer Him praise and commit themselves to righteousness that they might find eternal life. They have been commanded to abide by His law. Only man, among all of his many creations, can willfully depart from the law of his creator.

21:20 For the Lord has commanded of those who abide in righteousness- to hold fast and keep his law.

21:21 Man is granted his place by the Lord, who has placed crowns upon each of his creatures, upon the wild beasts of the land and the birds of heaven.

21:22 Whether they are found upon the sea or in the land, the Lord destroyed the whole of the created world upon their father, Adam. The Lord did this, so that they might live in his love, that they might eat the grain that grows upon the earth, that man might govern [the beasts] and that they might be commanded by the will of man. [The Lord] appointed those to govern his creation, that they might be guided by the commands of the Lord, who grants them their dignity and honors.

21:23 If they drift from His law, [the Lord] will snatch away the sovereignty He granted them. Since He is the king of the heavens and the earth, He will give it to those who do His will.

21:24 He has appointed those whom He loves and sacks all those who dismiss Him. It is [the Lord] that kills and saves, He that gives the lash in tribulation, and He that grants pardon.

21:25 There is no other God like Him[159], as he is sovereign over the whole of creation. He is Lord, and there are no peers to Him, either in the heavens

---

[159] This is an allusion to the precept of monotheism expressed in the Hebrew Bible (Deut 6:4). However, contextually it contends with the existence of other gods, something which would be present in the field work of early Ethiopian missionaries.

above or upon the earth below. There are none who sit in judgment above Him.

21:26 He alone crowns; He alone casts away; He lashes in tribulation; He pardons; He weakens, and He grants majesty. [160]

21:27 He hears the prostrations and pleas of man. He listens to the pleas of those who work His will with a pure heart. He hears their prayers and offers favor to those that supplicate of Him.

21:28 [The Lord] created them, the great and small, to be governed. This is their great wealth which sits upon the hills and summits, and in the roots and caverns beneath the well of the earth, and upon all their kin, in the land and sea.

21:29 For those men who do the will of God, this is their wealth. He will not take from their abundance, granting them only gifts and accolades.

21:30 [The Lord] shall bestow upon them the majesty that was prepared in heaven for their ancestors- Isaac, Abraham and Jacob. He shall offer them the reward granted to Hezekiah, David and Samuel, who did not break the law of the Lord, or disobey His commands.

21:31 They, therefore, will rejoice in his sovereignty. [The Lord] will grant to them the glory of the ages, the great dignity prepared for their fathers: Isaac, Abraham, and Jacob. For [the Lord] has promised to guard their inheritance.

Chapter XXII:
Judgments of the Lord

22:1 Please remember the names of those who were committed to good deeds, and do not forget their actions[161].

22:2 Recant your former ways, that your name might be regarded as theirs is, and that you might rejoice with the [saints] in the Kingdom of Heaven. There in the abode of light, [the Lord] has prepared for princes and kings who did the will of the Lord and were righteous.

22:3 Again, know and remember the names of wicked kings and princes, for among men [the Lord] shall convict and censure them after they have died.

22:4 For they did not commit to the forward path, which they saw and heard. Know and remember, that unless they did the will of the Lord, He shall pass His sentencing upon them in the Kingdom of Heaven, just as He does with sinners who forget the law of the Lord.

22:5 Be gentle, innocent and honest; yet, do not follow those who forget the law of the Lord, with whom the Lord is displeased because of the deeds done by their hands.

22:6 Discern the truth, protect the orphans and the widows from those sinners who seek to rob them.

22:7 Protect the orphans, save them from the rich man who seeks to exploit him. Stand for them

---

[160] The redundancy here appears to be for dramatic inflection intending to emphasize the moral value of divine sovereignty to the audience.

[161] This vocative address appears to be the start of another sermon. Moreover, its direction would be consistent following the commemoration of saints within the early Christian liturgy.

and offer them the proper care. If not, you will find yourselves in the lake of fire[162], where unrepentant sinners are punished.

22:8 Straighten yourself towards the ways of love and the path of justice. For the eyes of the Lord fall upon His friends, and His ears hear their supplications. Pursue this love and follow it.

22:9 The Lord shall direct the face of his wrath upon all those who are committed to evil deeds, so that none might evoke their name upon the earth. He will not save one, whether they abide within battlements or upon the mountains.

22:10 For I am the Lord, who is a jealous god, and I am a God who takes vengeance. I destroy those who have revulsion to Me and ignore my word. To them I will not show My continence, or offering any aide, for I will annihilate them.

22:11 I will show favor to those who honor Me and keep My word.

Chapter XXIII:
Those Who Follow the Path of Cain

23:1 Do not walk in the ways of Cain, who killed his innocent brother, who walked beside him, for he believed that his brother loved him.

23:2 He killed his brother for he had great jealous for his wife, for those who are envious of their neighbor walk in the ways [of Cain], full of sin and betrayal.

23:3 Since Abel was an innocent lamb, his blood is akin to the unspotted lamb sacrificed to the Lord by the pure of heart. Those who are not upon the path of Abel, walk upon the path of Cain.

23:4 Those people who abide in virtue are those who experience the love of God, just as Abel the just did. For they are virtuous just as Abel was. They abide in the deeds of Abel, who loved the Lord.

23:5 Yet, the Lord shows his total disregard to those who are evil. He casts His terrible judgment upon them and upon their flesh. It is written upon their hearts[163], and when they are convicted, their sentence will be pronounced before all mankind, before the angels and the whole of the world.

23:6 They shall know their disgrace, the sinful and the proud, and all those who did not do the will of the Lord shall come to disgrace.

23:7 Words of caution will be granted to them, saying 'they shall go into Gehenna, where there is no respite for eternity.'

Chapter XXIV:
The Hazards of Idolatry

24:1 In ages past, Gideon had trust in the Lord, and he defeated the armies of the uncircumcised. They were numerous, an army of tens of

---

[162] See Rev. 20:14

[163] See Jer. 31:33

thousands, which moved like the countless locusts of the air.

24:2 prince and kings! Since there is no God beside me[164], do not put faith in the sundry idols.

24:3 For I am your God, the Lord, who sent you forth from your mother's womb[165], who raised, fed and clothed you. For what reason do you excuse yourselves? Why do you offer praise to the idols, and ignore Me?

24:4 I have done all of this for your benefit, but for what have you given Me? It is for you to abide under My law, as I have commanded, so that you may maintain the state of your flesh. Still, there is nothing I have requested?

24:5 The Lord, who is king, has said "Save yourselves from the worship of idols, from the practice of sorcery[166] and from welcoming doubt into your hearts."

24:6 The wrath of the Lord shall fall upon those who are committed to this, and upon those who listen to [these transgressors] and do their will. All those who are their companions and abide by their beliefs, help yourselves, do not praise those idols.

24:7 There are people who are unknown to you and show no favor to you. They shall rise up against you unless you have the fear of the Lord's will. They will consume the wealth you have labored for[167]. Just as His servant the prophets spoke, and Enoch[168] and

Asaph[169] also spoke, "unless you do the will of the Lord, they will consume your wealth and your labor."

24:8 An evil man will appear before you after changing his garments and say, "There is no law to govern me." They, therefore, live in sin in all they do, feasting and adorning themselves with instruments of silver and gold, and committing the deeds that are detestable to the Lord.

24:9 Yet. Those who are prepared for the feast, after they have been awoken from their sleep in the morning, up until the hours of the evening, they commit evil deeds. They live in perdition in their ways, for they do not walk in the path of charity.

24:10 They do not know love in their deeds, for there is no fear of the Lord upon their continence. They are wicked ones, who hold no religion or virtue. They are covetous, taking their meals alone. They are given to drink and their sin is unbounded by the law. They are lecherous, violent, thieving, and lying. They steal from the poor.

24:11 They offer rebuke without charity, and without the law, for they do not fear the Lord their Creator. Upon their continence there is no fear.

24:12 There is no shame in their faces when they are seen. They are not perturbed by their grey hair or their aging continence. They can be heard

---

[164] See Deut. 4:35; Is. 45:5
[165] Jer. 1:5
[166] Gal. 5:19-21; 2 Chr. 33:6
[167] An inversion of a Hebrew blessing Ps. 128:2
[168] While Enoch is noted in the Genesis account (5:19-21), his fame is derived from the text of 1

Enoch, another canonical book of the Ethiopian scriptures.
[169] He is likely referencing the Psalmist, Asaph, who was said to have been a contemporary of King David. However, Enoch quoting Asaph is chronologically impossible.

saying, "There is great wealth in this world!" They make this wealth for themselves, before they can even see it. They have no fear of the Lord upon their faces. And when the rich can cast their eyes upon their gains, it has already vanished.

24:13 Those men consume their wealth. They are full of hypocrisy, and their rests nothing true upon their tongues. They do not perform at dusk what they spoke of at daybreak.

24:14 They ignore the pleas of the poor and suffering. Those monarchs work for what is evil, stalking the [neglected], and not offering asylum to the alien, who is robbed by the rich.

24:15 Let [the kings] protect those who have been wronged and the alien. Let the monarchs not be afraid of evoking justice.

24:16 All those who extort gold, who rob a man of his wealth, they are offenders, for their deeds are wicked. They are cruel when they eat a newborn calf with its mother, and a mother-bird with its egg[170]. They make everyone see and hear the extent of their wealth.

24:17 They love to horde for themselves, ignoring the poor and the sick. They forcibly take money from those who have none, and collect their fortunes together, so that they might celebrate and become plump.

24:18 They shall perish without hesitation, like a dung-beetle[171] that comes forth from its pit, who cannot discern its own tracks, and cannot return whence it came. Woe unto their bodies on that day, for because they did not commit themselves to righteous deeds in this life, the Lord will be disturbed and take hold of them.

24:19 On that day, the Lord will ignore them, and they will fall at once into the pit of expiation. He will not act quickly to destroy them, observing their deeds in hopes of repentance. Yet, they shall perish when the time is appointed to them.

24:20 If they do not change and repent, He will decimate them just as He has to those who came before, who did not observe the law and give what is expected.

24:21 All those who consume the flesh and drink of the blood of a man[172], committing to vicious deeds have truly sinned. Upon their continence there is no fear of the Lord. From the hour they arise from their beds, the do not find respite in their sinfulness.

24:22 Their deeds are their sustenance, and they are weighed down by their sin. For they seek to destroy the

---

[170] This is a dietary law specified in Ex. 23:19. It is perhaps odd that this Kosher resistrion is noted here, as it would not have been closely observed by Christians in the 4th century.

[171] Or more literally, a "scarab". For this reason it might have been intended to have a double-meaning, as Scarabs were a common amulet with Egyptian mythology. They would have been in decreased popularity in this period, but still indefinitely linked to pagan belief.

[172] This is a violation of the prohibition on cannibalism (Deut. 28:53-57; Lev. 26:29; 2 Ki. 6:26-29; Jer. 19:9; Lam. 4:10). Why the author sought to include this is obscured, but it was likely a concern that was present in their congregation. In southern Ethiopia, there is the presense of the Me'en people who do engage in this practice historically. However, it would be impossible to discern if this was true in late antiquity as well.

bodies of the men of this world.

Chapter XXV:

25:1 Since their deeds are unjust, and as those who abide in Satan's work are misled, the Lord who rules all has said, "Woe unto your flesh and upon the hour that I am displeased and seize it."

25:2 Therefore, they do not know the Lord and his deeds. They have neglected the past and ignored My law.

25:3 In the days of fulfilment, I will bring tribulation upon them for their wicked deeds because I have recorded their sins. I will take vengeance and decimate them upon My day of judgment[173].

25:4 I, the Lord, am complete from vista to vista, and all creation rests under My sovereignty. There are none who escape from my rule, neither in the heavens or upon the earth, nor within the depths of the seas.

25:5 It is I who command the snake that resides below the earth[174], and I who order the fish of the sea. I set forth the birds of the heavens and of the camels who abide in the wilderness. For this is My possession, everything that is marked across the horizon.

25:6 It is I who perform untold deeds and can work miracles.

Upon the heavens and the earth, there is none who is beyond My sovereignty. There is no one to whom I can say, "Where are you going? What do you do?"

25:7 I command the angels, their captains and divisions. All of creation, I call by name, as my possessions. The beasts of the desert, the birds of the air and all the creatures are my wealth.

25:8 It will come with the movement of the locust and appear in the droughts or the east. In the days of fulfillment, the Red Sea shall become quiet, and the Lord shall arise towards her, in fear and eminence.

25:9 For He rules the living and the dead,[175] and she will cease being heard, along the country of Sabea[176], and Nubia, India and Ethiopia, and all the their boundaries.

25:10 He observes all in His great authority and purity. For His glory surpasses all others. He keeps communities under His protection.

25:11 [The Lord's] power is greater than all other powers, for His kingdom surpasses all other kingdoms. It is His authority that is sovereign over the earth, for He stands overall and there is nothing that is beyond Him.

25:12 He reigns over the clouds of the heavens. He gives grass for the livestock to grow upon the

---

[173] See Rom. 12:19

[174] This is a curious statement, as it appears that the author is familiar with the 'Drakon Aithiopikos'. That is to say, they have heard of the Greek legend of the serpant who is native to the lands of Ethiopia. The ancient Greek zoologist, Aelian, writing in the 2nd century, makes note of this creature (*On Animals 2.21*), although he appears to have never visited sub-saharan africa. From this we might assume that our author was immersed in Hellenic culture and was not a native to Ethiopia proper.

[175] See Rom. 14:9

[176] Or rather, Arabia, as this is an archaic title for that country.

earth and lets the fruit blossom forth.

25:13 He feeds all of those which He loves. He sustains all those which He created, by fruits and nourishment. He sustains the insects and locusts underneath the earth, and the beasts and creatures upon it. For all those who pray, He listens to their prayer. He does not ignore the pleas of the orphan or the widow.

25:14 The upheaval of evil men is like a tornado, and the counsel of wicked men is akin to murky urine. [The Lord] will accept the prayers of those, the pure, who go to Him.

25:15 The flesh vanishes like one of the birds of heaven, and the beauty of silver and gold are fleeting in this world. Yet, judgment will meet those who remember their gold, but forget the law of God. Their fine garments will be consumed by moths;

25:16 and beetles will devour their storehouse[177] of barley and wheat. They too shall pass away, just as those who came before did. For just as words that proceed from the mouth can never return, a sinner who loves only money can love no other. Their beautiful existence is just a passing shadow, and their wealth before the Lord is meaningless.

25:17 Yet, if generosity is shown, the Lord will not turn away from them. They will be granted favor for their charity to the neglected and their care for those orphaned. The Lord will listen to those who do not neglect the needs of children,

or the alien sufferer, and who clothe the naked in the robes that the Lord has given them[178].

25:18 They do not show their favor to only those they know, nor place the lowly above their peers. They observe the truth of the Lord, just as a double-bladed sword. They do not plant iniquity in their harvests, nor in the weights of their balances.

Chapter XXVI:
The Judgment of Rich and Poor Alike

26:1 Before they sleep, the poor will think twice, for if the rich do not receive them, then they will become like dead wood, that can produce no greenery. For the roots cannot be fertile where there is no moisture, and the leaves will not come forth if there is no root.

26:2 The leaves must serve the flower, the adornment of the fruit; yet unless the leaves are fertile, it will not bear fruit[179], just as a man without religion has no virtue.

26:3 However, if he abides by his faith, he will have virtue, for the Lord rejoices in a man who commits to true and honest work.

26:4 To those men who have pleaded with Him, [the Lord] will grant the requests spoken by their tongues. He will never castigate the honest man because of the work that he has done.

26:5 Since the Lord is just, and He loves the deeds of the just, He

---

[177] See Ps. 78:45
[178] Matt. 25:36

[179] See Matt. 12:33; Lu. 6:43-45

will not accept the sinner without their due penance for the evil they have wrought. The souls of all men lie under the rule of [the Lord], for He is the one who is sovereign over the heavens and the earth. He will not show favor to the rich any more then to the poor on the day of judgment. He will not welcome those without repentance.

Chapter XXVII:

27:1 It was He, [the Lord], that has made every being, and bestowed life unto his creatures. He set the form of the mountains and hills and cast the waters upon the earth. He separated the sea from the land. And with His first word, He brought forth light[180].

27:2 Because this world was covered in darkness, He created the light. He brought forth all creation, molding this world and setting its course with its wealth and order. He spoke, "Let it become dark in the evening".

27:3 The Lord again spoke for light to come forth, and there was daybreak, and He raised the water up above the earth.

27:4 He stretched out the heavens like a tent[181], and He supported it with the winds. He placed the waters underneath the earth.

27:5 [The Lord] formed the sea separate from the land, and made it solid by His power, so that no creature might drown in the waters. He placed the wild beasts upon the earth. Leviathan and Behemoth[182], who were massive creatures, He set forth within the earth itself. Upon the earth He placed an untold number of creatures, both seen and unseen.

27:6 On the third day, the Lord created plants upon the earth, and all those things which bear fruit, roots, and wood. The fruit of the earth He made beautiful in His sight.

27:7 He made the fruit of the earth beautiful for man to see and sweet for him to eat. [The Lord] created the grass, and all vegetation that produces seeds to be food for birds, cattle, and wild beasts.

27:8 The sun rose and set, and on the fourth day [the Lord] said "Let there be light in the heavens (called "cosmos")[183]. After the Lord created the moon, and the sun, and the stars, He placed them in the heavens (called "cosmos") so that they might shine over the earth and offer light in the darkness.

27:9 After this, the moon, the sun, and the stars shifted twilight to starlight.

27:10 On the fifth day the Lord created all the creatures that reside within the waters, and all the birds of the heavens,

---

[180] See Gen. 1:3

[181] See Ps. 104:2

[182] This reference does not appear in the Book of Genesis but is an allusion to two creatures mentioned late in the Book of Job. Our author appears familiar with these two mythical creatures but has interjected them into his reading of the Genesis account.

[183] This doesn't appear to be an intended to be an original part of the sermon. However, the introjection of the Greek word 'cosmos', does seem to suggest that the author was from the Greek speaking world and sought to import Hellenic cosmology to his listeners.

and of all those creatures seen and unseen.

27:11 On the sixth day, [the Lord] created cattle, wild beasts and all those [that abide upon the earth]. The Lord, having created them all, and setting forth a place for them, created Adam in his image and likeness.

27:12 [The Lord] gave him all the creatures which he fashioned so that he might govern over them- all those cattle, wild beasts and sea creatures, and upon Leviathan and Behemoth that reside in the sea.

27:13 He gave him all the quadrupeds of the earth, and the livestock, and the creatures both seen and unseen.

27:14 [The Lord] placed Adam, whom he fashioned in His image and likeness, in the garden, so that He might eat and nurture the plant life and offer praise to the Lord.

27:15 So that he might not disobey the command [of the Lord], He said to him, "If you eat of this fig tree[184], you will experience death."

27:16 [The Lord] commanded him so that he might not eat of the fig tree that brings only death and draws the budding of good and evil.

27:17 Our mother, Eve, was coerced in this by the serpent, who misled her. She ate of this fig tree and gave it to our father, Adam.

27:18 And Adam, having eaten from the fig tree, brought death down upon himself and upon his children.

27:19 Since [Adam] disobeyed [the Lord's] ordinances, eating from the fig tree that the Lord prohibited, saying "do not eat from her." The Lord was displeased with our father, Adam, and expelled him from the garden, sending him into exile. [The Lord] gave him the land that produced thistles and thorns and cursed him for disobey His commandment. He thereafter had to toil in weariness, plowing the earth for his sustenance.

27:20 When the Lord sent him forth to this land, Adam was filled with melancholy. He toiled in his labors, plowing the earth for grain, and began his tiresome drudgery.

Chapter XXVIII:

28:1 After his children grew and multiplied, there were some who gave glory and praise to the Lord and abided by His commandments.

28:2 There arose prophets who spoke on what has been and what will be to come; and from his children there were sinners who spoke lies and who harmed others. Cain, the firstborn of Adam, accepted evil and slayed his brother, Abel[185].

28:3 The Lord was troubled by the earth, because she consumed blood, and He cast His judgment upon Cain because he had murdered his brother, Abel.

---

[184] This is replaying the events of Genesis 2:17, with the added detail that this was a fig tree, which the original text of Genesis does not state. Elsewhere in the apocrypha of the Ethiopian Bible the tree is described as being "very-fine grapes" (1 Enoch 31:4). Our author must not have been familiar with this account.
[185] See Gen. 4:8

28:4 The Lord asked Cain, "Where is your brother, Abel? "To which Cain, in his arrogance, said "Am I my brother Abel's keeper?"[186]

28:5 Abel was transformed into an unblemished one, but Cain became a sinner through the act of killing an innocent man, Abel, his brother.

28:6 Another child, the gentle Seth was born, for Adam was father of sixty children[187].

28:7 They are gentle people from this line, those who were prophets and those who were sinners and betrayers.

28:8 There are those blessed people who do the work of their father, Adam, in accordance with his will. For he told his child, Seth, to keep the law of the Lord, from the days of Adam until those of Noah.

28:9 [Adam] passed the law of the Lord on to his progeny, saying to them, "Stand on guard". [He said] not to destroy the law of the Lord, to pass it to their children, just as Noah their father did, keeping the law of the Lord.

28:10 Thereafter, they abided, teaching their children and all those born after them.

28:11 Satan also resided when [the Lord] spoke to their fathers, having abided in the idols of the dead which have curses upon them. He defeated these people, and they did all that Satan, their teacher, requested of them.

28:12 They resided in the world where the idols were worshipped, until the gentle Abraham, who did the will of the Lord.

28:13 He had resided in the law of the Lord, being different from his kin. Therefore, the Lord swore an oath to him, having come in wind and in fire.

28:14 The Lord made his promise that He might grant a land for [Abraham's] children to inherit up until the days of eternity.

28:15 [The Lord again] swore to Isaac, promising him the inheritance of his father Abraham. He too swore to Jacob that he might possess Isaac's inheritance. He made this oath like he had to Isaac.

28:16 [The Lord] then divided his children, born after that of Jacob into the twelve tribes of Israel. He made them kings and priests and blessed them saying "flourish and be fruitful."[188]

28:17 He granted them their father's inheritance. Yet, while He fed them and loved them, they did not stop in offending the Lord.

28:18 Thereafter, He decimated them, and they will seek Him in their prayer. They will repent and find the Lord, and He shall grant them His clemency.

28:19 For He shows His kindness upon his creation. He shall show pardon because of the deeds of their fathers who loved Him, not for their own sake.

28:20 [The Lord] shall stretch forth His bountiful right hand which will satiate their hunger. He will show His mercy and multiply their grain harvest.

---

[186] See Gen. 4:9

[187] This number stands in contrast to other Hebrew folklore. Flavius Josephus by comparison states that Adam was father to thirty-three sons (Antiq. 1.2.2).

[188] See Gen. 1:28

28:21 He gives sustenance to the nestlings and the wild beasts who supplicate of Him. When they plead to Him, He will save the children of Israel from the hands of their enemies, holding them back.

28:22 Yet, they will again embrace iniquity and perturb [the Lord], and He will send forth their enemy nations. They will destroy them, slaughtering and seizing them.

28:23 They will shout to the Lord in mourning and consternation. By the hand of the prophets did He send help and save his people.

28:24 There were also times when He saved them through the deeds of princes. For they had grieved the Lord, and their adversaries had tithed and oppressed them.

28:25 David had arisen and spared them from the deeds of the Philistines. Yet, they still offended the Lord, so He sent upon them people to oppress them.

28:26 Again, there were times when [the Lord] saved them through the deeds of Jephthah[189], but they forgot the Lord who spared their times of tribulation. Since the Lord has brought destitution upon them, He will send forth the wickedness of their enemies, who will subjugate them.

28:27 At that time, they were oppressed by the trial upon them. They cried to the Lord, and He sent His salvation by the hands of Gideon. Yet, they

grieved the Lord by the work of their hands.

28:28 He again sent forth nations who cast tribulations upon them. They again returned to the Lord, begging and weeping.

28:29 Yet again, he saved them from the nations through the works of Samson, and they took rest from their suffering. However, they dwelled in the fear of the Lord for their former sins.

28:30 The Lord sent upon them other nations which were unconcerned for their welfare. They prayed to the Lord again, crying and weeping to Him, that He might send aid to them. He saved them from the nations by the deeds of Barak and Deborah.

28:31 Again, a short season passed, and they worshiped the Lord. They offended the Lord and adopted their former sins, offending His person.

28:32 And He sent upon them other people to concern them, and again saved them by the hand of Judith[190]. Yet, after a brief interregnum, they again offended the Lord with their sin as they had done previously.

28:33 He sent against them [foreign] people to rule over them. At this they wept to the Lord, for He had touched Abimelech[191] the warrior on his forehead, so that he might battle in the lands of Judah.

28:34 [The Lord] saved them by the hand of Mattathiah[192] and his children. When that warrior

---

[189] This biblical figure is said to have reigned over Israel for six years (Jud. 12:7). However, it is not clear why the author sought to use him as an example of the repetition of sin and redemption in the Hebrew Scriptures.

[190] Judith of Bethulia, who is the prmary heroine of the apocryphal 'Book of Judith'

[191] See Jud. 9:1-6

[192] This is the only standing reference to the Maccabee family in the text. As Mattathiah, and his sons, are credited with starting the revolt against Seleucid authority in the region (1 Mac. 2:1). It stands to reason that the author had access to the

died, his army retreated and dissolved. The children of Israel followed them and battled them into the [river] Jabbok[193]. They did not spare even one among them.

28:35 After some time had passed, they arose and troubled the Lord, and He sent peoples over them to rule them. Again, they cried to the Lord, who ignored their pleas and mourning, for they distressed the Lord on each occasion and had destroyed His law.

28:36 They were taken as hostages with their priests into the land of the Babylonians.

28:37 Then, the children of Israel, who had betrayed the Lord, did not stop their offenses, committing sin and worshipping their idols.

28:38 The Lord was disturbed that He should destroy them for their iniquity. Haman deposited ten thousand gold pieces in the royal treasury and waited for the day to act accordingly. (He incited anger in the mind of King Ahasuerus, so that he could not preserve the children [of Israel] in the land of Persia, from India to Ethiopia, and pushed him to annihilate them.)

28:39 [Haman] did accordingly, and he wrote a letter under the king's authority. He was given the royal seal that he might send his message across the land of Persia.

28:40 The seal was given to him so that he might exterminate them all on a single day upon orders of the king. He was able to entice [the king] so that

their wealth, their gold and silver, might be taken and placed in the king's treasury.

28:41 When the children of Israel heard this, they wept and cried to the Lord. They pleaded to Mordecai, and Mordecai pleaded to Esther[194].

28:42 Esther spoke, saying "Children of Israel- Fast! Supplicate! Cry out to the Lord in all the lands where you reside!"

28:43 Thereafter, Mordecai dressed in sackcloth and placed dust upon himself. The children of Israel fasted and begged, entering into penitence in all the lands where they dwelled.

28:44 Esther fell into despair. Being a queen, she also dressed in sackcloth and placed dust upon her head and shaved it. She did not anoint her body with perfume in the manner of the Queens of Persia. In the depths of her soul she cried, weeping to her father, the Lord God.

28:45 Since [Esther] loved Him alongside the King of Persia, Ahasuerus, she prepared a meal for her father, the Creator.

28:46 When Haman and the king entered for the meal that Esther had prepared, he showed his love upon her and upon Mordecai. Therefore, the Lord laid out hardship upon Haman, and they hung him from a high tree.

28:47 The king sent more that they might release the Israelites and grant them full pardon. They granted that they should not be fined, robbed, or deprived of their former property.

---

text of Maccabees if he saw the need to offer commentary upon it.

[193] Now known as the Zarqa river. This battle is otherwise unknown to history.
[194] See Est. 4:1-17

28:48 The Lord sent his reprieve to the Israelites, for they cried and repented accordingly at that time. This was done so that they might love and honor them in the land of Persia. The letter of the king went forth, sparing them from the annihilation of their nation and the plundering of their wealth.

28:49 It was at this time that they saddened [the Lord]. He therefore will prepare [a tribulation] upon those peoples. On that day, they will weep and call out that the Lord send forth an advocate, that he might spare them from the deeds of the nations who persecute them.

Chapter XXIX:

29:1 When the Egyptians enslaved the children of Israel, they made them make bricks in haste. [The Israelites] toiled by setting mud in straw and cooking bricks[195].

29:2 During that time, they forced this labor upon them, setting captains to pace the many workers. [The Hebrews] cried to the Lord, that He might spare them from the toil of setting bricks for the Egyptians.

29:3 [The Lord] sent Aaron and Moses to them to aid them. The Lord sent them so that they might bring their kin out from under the sovereignty of Pharaoh. He spared them from the working of bricks. In [the pharaoh's] arrogance, he repudiated any attempt to release the Israelites, so that they could not make sacrifices and be governed by the Lord in the wilderness. The Lord then sent [the Israelites] forth and sent his [angels][196] against the King of Egypt, upon his royal palace, so that they might be spared.

29:4 For the Lord ignores the arrogant and has drowned the pharaoh in the Eritrean Sea[197] with his army because of his pride.

29:5 For just like [Pharaoh], [the Lord] shall decimate those who govern their kingdoms wickedly, as the Lord has properly granted them their crown. All those princes and king who ignore the word of the Lord should act in accord with justice. In turn they should appoint those who will serve in righteous deeds and grant them their just due, so that they all might honor the name of the Lord.

29:6 The Lord, the King of universe says "If they will repent their rule, I will aid their sovereignty.

29:7 Commit to righteousness, and I shall perform great deeds for you. Keep My law and I shall protect your life. Live in commitment to the law and I shall grant you trustworthiness and peace in your heart.

---

[195] Curiously, this detail is not found in the Hebrew Bible, which only noted that the Hebrew slaves built cities for the Egyptians. This means of making mud-brick, while common in Egypt, was not used for state construction projects. Government work were frequently made of stone, an accessible commodity in the African desert. However, this detail does offer insight into the writer, who would have been familiar with the agrarian use of mud-bricks along Nile civilizations.

[196] This meaning is obscured by the passage, as it is unclear who the Lord sent against the pharaoh. In this context it might understood to be the 'Angel of Death', but that is only understood in the context of Exodus and does not appear directly in this text.

[197] Alternatively known as the Red Sea

29:8 Love [the Lord], and I shall protect you, reside with me and I shall restore you."

29:9 The Lord, the King of the universe, says, "Take faith in Me, and I shall spare you from this trial."

29:10 Do not abide together, as the Lord, the ruler of mankind, loves honest deeds. The Lord says, "When you come to Me, I will come to you. All those who are sinners and betrayers, cleanse yourself from iniquity and repent of your evil thoughts.

29:11 I shall hold back My anger against you, and instead I will bring to you charity and clemency.

29:12 I shall banish the wicked and unjust from My sight. For I saved my servant, David, from his enemies who sought his life in their malice, from Goliath's war-like hands, from the works of Saul, who sought to kill him, and from his son Absalom's plots, who wished to usurp his kingdom.

29:13 I shall save all those who keep My law and do My will. I will grant them majesty and they will rejoice in this world and in the world to come. I shall place a crown on them, that they might be just."

29:14 They shall stand like those kings who served the Lord [in the past], and had honor bestowed upon them for their deeds. [They will stand] as the prophet Samuel, who served God with dignity, from his nativity to death, and elected to stand with the Lord and His laws.

29:15 [The Lord] spoke to him, so they he might serve Eli the priest, who served the Lord

and abided in the temple. Samuel did these deeds, and showed his great mercy, and for this he was beloved.

29:16 He then grew and served in the house of the Lord, the temple. He was appointed and anointed by [the Lord], so that he might too appoint over the people kings that might perform the will of the Lord. Since the Lord has loved His people, He had appointed one among the children of Israel. When He had fulfilled the Lord's will, who created him, He was anointed over the kingdom by his hand.

29:17 When Saul reigned in his kingdom, the Lord said to the prophet Samuel "Go, for I have found favor in the son of Jesse, David, who was born among the children of Judah. Anoint him."[198]

Chapter XXX:
The Sovereignty of God

30:1 "I revile the children of [King] Saul, for he offended Me because of his violation of My word.

30:2 I abandoned him for he did not observe the law, and I will not offer the crown to his descendants again.

30:3 Those who do not keep My law and My word are as he is. I shall exile them and their children from the gifts of My kingdom until the days of eternity.

30:4 Since they did nor praised Me in the days I raised them up, I shall eradicate them, and I will

[198] See 1 Sam. 16:1-13

never again make them great. While I shall honor them, even though they have not honored Me, I will bestow greatness upon them.

30:5 They did not act in charity when I showed My charity to them, they did not forgive, though I granted them forgiveness.

30:6 They did not make Me their rightful sovereign, though I made them a king upon the nations, and they showed no dignity to Me, though I gave them great majesty over all people. I will not give them majesty or bestow honor upon them for they have not observed My law.

30:7 I shall withhold the gifts I have given them, and remove the wealth they had previously attained, for they have disturbed Me by their oath." The Lord, the Ruler of the universe, spoke "I will honor those who honor Me, and love those who love Me.

30:8 I will disperse all those who did not observe My law from the gifts I have bestowed upon them."

30:9 The Lord, the ruler of the universe, spoke, saying "I love those who love me, and I praise those who praise me.

30:10 For I am the Lord, who is sovereign over the universe; there is no one who is beyond My power in heaven or upon the earth. I am He who gives life and takes it, who brings grief and pardon.

30:11 Renown and righteousness are My wealth and I grant them to whom I wish. For I am the great judge and the

executioner. I make lowly all those who displease Me.

30:12 And I am He who grants pardon to those whom I love and call upon My name. I am He who nourishes both rich and poor.

30:13 I feed the birds of the air and the fish of the sea, the wild beasts and all the flowers, for I feed more than just mankind.

30:14 I give nourishment to crocodiles, to whales, to gophers, badgers, and hippopotamus,

30:15 And to all the creatures that reside in the water and fly upon the wind. For I do not feed man alone. This is My wealth.

30:16 I am He who nourished those who search for Me, for they are the just and beloved."

Chapter XXXI:
The Just Rule of Kings

31:1 "Kings cannot reign without My consent. Nor can suffering come without My command. Men cannot be poor unless I have charged it as such, nor can authorities maintain their power without My will. For they have no authority without My will[199].

31:2 I granted such favor to My beloved David, just as wisdom was given to Solomon and I gave years of life to Hezekiah[200].

31:3 I extinguished the life of Goliath and gave strength to Sampson. Yet, I also took his strength from him[201].

[199] See Jn. 19:11
[200] See 2 Ki. 20:6

[201] See Jud. 16:28-30

31:4   I saved My servant David from the hand of Goliath the warrior.

31:5   And later, I saved him from the hand of King Saul, and from another warrior[202] who was his enemy. Since [David] kept my commands, I saved him from those who opposed him and his enemies.

31:6   I have loved [David], just as I love all those princes and kings who observe My law. They have given delight to Me, and for this I will let them abide in majesty over their foes.

31:7   They might be heirs to the land of their forefathers. I will grant them the spotless country to inherit that I promised to their ancestors[203]."

Chapter XXXII:
The Sustaining Providence of the Lord

32:1   The Lord, who is sovereign, said, "You princes and king, hear this, my word, and keep my commands. For you have caused me to grieve, just as I had when the children of Israel worshipped their sundry idols. I, the Lord who created them, have protected them and saved them." The Lord who reigns, spoke, saying "Hear my word! All you whom I have fed and raised, all those whom I have loved since they were born to your parents.

32:2   All those whom I have sent to work the harvests of the earth, and whom I have sustained out of the fat of the land, they to whom I have given the grapevine and the ripe fruit of the olive tree, and the clear waters of ancient wells,

32:3   Hear my word! Before you offend me as the children of Israel did when they worshipped their idols when they knew that I, the Lord, was their creator." He said to them, "Who gave them milk and honey[204] with farro? Who has clothed them with garments? Who has given to them the fullness of their love?

32:4   If they were deprived of this sustenance, they would again beg it from Me."

Chapter XXXIII:
The Temporality of Earthly Rule

33:1   David spoke, saying "The children of Israel were fed manna that was deposited by the angels."[205] "Listen again to My word, so that you too do not offend Me just as the children of Israel did when they worshipped idols. I am their God, the Lord, who gave them sweet manna in the wilderness to eat." [The Lord] said, "I performed all of this for them so that they might offer me just and worthy praise."

33:2   The Lord, the Ruler of the universe, said "Regardless, they have not worshipped Me, and therefore I have ignored them. They have offended Me, and have abided by the law of the idols, which is not My law.

---

[202] Prince Absalom or King Achish of Gath
[203] See Deut. 30:5

[204] See Ex. 33:3
[205] See Ex. 16:35

33:3   Therefore, I will bring tribulation upon them for their sin, as they have refused worship and have not abided under my counsel and order. Therefore, I have ignored their welfare because of the iniquity committed by their hands. I shall cast them down into Gehenna into the terrible judgment that can only be rendered in the heavens.

33:4   Since they have not kept the law and since I am troubled by mankind, I shall reduce their time in this world.

33:5   If you be a king, are you not also a man who will die, who will vanish and tomorrow become nothing but dust and maggots?

33:6   Yet, this day you boast and are full of pride as if you will live forever.

33:7   The Lord, the ruler of the universe, has said, "You who think that you are healthy this day, might be the man who finds death tomorrow.

33:8   However, if you keep My commands and My word, I will grant to you an honored nation with greatness residing in My will. Their palaces will be radiant, and their crowns will be magnificent. Their thrones shall be composed of silver and gold, ornamented for those who sit upon [the throne].

33:9   And they shall rejoice, all those within that nation, filled with people committed to moral deeds.

33:10   Yet, for those people who are sinful and do not abide under the law" said the Lord, ruler of the universe

33:11   "It is not proper that they should pass into that nation where rightful kings dwell."

Chapter XXXIV:
The Fate of the Table of Nations

34:1   The kingdom of Media shall vanish, and Rome will be built upon the foundations of the Macedonian kingdom. The kingdom of Nineveh[206] will built upon the foundation of the Persian kingdom.

34:2   The kingdom of Ethiopia will be built upon the foundation of the Alexandrian kingdom[207]. As the people will arise and the kingdom of Moab will be built upon the foundations of the Amalekite kingdom[208].

34:3   Brother will arise against brother and Lord shall take His vengeance, His decimation will be cast against them, for He has spoken this.

---

[206] This appears to be an allusion to the decimation of the former Parthian state, which was replaced with the centralized Sassanid Empire. It's capital, Seleucia-Ctesiphon, like the historic city of Ninevah, was a Mesopotamian citadel.

[207] This appears to be part of the political and military ambition present in Ethiopia during the composition of this text. St. Ezana, King of Axum, who reigned in the 4th century, did appear to have a similar ambition in his northern campaigns, subduing nubain lands that stood on the boarder with the Roman Empire. Moreover, it is during St.

Ezana's reign that Ethiopia officially converts to Christianity.

[208] The Kebra Negast 79 appears to build upon this mistaken premise that the biblical figure of Ammon is the father of the Amalekites. This short tractate associates contemporary political powers with their historic tribal affiliations. In this instance, this kingdom to the east of the Jordan river appears to be the Ghassanid kingdom which occupied much othe eastern Levant from the 3rd to 7th centuries. There presense in this text suggests that they had become the dominate power in the region when this was composed.

34:4 "Nation shall rise against nation[209], the one people shall fall upon another," [The Lord] has said.

34:5 Debate shall rage and there will be battles, famine and plague, earthquakes and drought[210]. Charity will perish from the earth, for the Lord's terrible punishment will fall upon them all.

34:6 The day when the dead shall proceed forth will come, prominent as the terror of lightening, striking east to west.

34:7 Upon the day when the Lord passes judgement all shall receive tribulation for the deeds wrought by his hands and because of the weight of his sin. For [the Lord] has said, "I shall take revenge."[211] On that day, their feet will be bound, for the day of their destruction will have arrived.

34:8 On that day, the Lord will forever annihilate all those who dwell in Gehenna, those who did not abide by His law and who did evil.

34:9 "All those who reside in the western islands[212], Nubia, India, Arabia and Ethiopia, as well as the people of Egypt, all people who abide there,

34:10 they shall all know that it is I, the Lord, who rule over the heavens and the earth, who grants honor and fame, who saves and who kills.

34:11 I am He who sends forth the Sun, who moves it towards it

twilight, who forges good and evil[213].

34:12 It is I who brings forth aliens, who slay and consume the wealth for which you have toiled, the sheep and cattle of your flocks.

34:13 They shall take your children hostage, and smash their heads before you, while you are unable to rescue them. Because the Holy Ghost[214] does not reside in you, and you have not feared the Lord's commands that you have heard, He shall destroy all your finery and possessions.

34:14 A person whom the Holy Ghost resides within will know all. Just as Nebuchadnezzar spoke to Daniel, saying "I have seen the spirit of the Lord dwelling within you"[215].

34:15 A man in whom the Holy Ghost dwells will know all. What has been hidden from him will be disclosed, as there is nothing that can be concealed from those whom the Holy Ghost dwells within.

34:16 Yet, as we are mortal people, who may die tomorrow, our sins and our deeds will be revealed.

34:17 Just as silver and gold are smelted in the fire, so shall sinners be upon the day of [His] arrival[216] when all will be examined, for they did not observe the Lord's commands.

---

[209] See Matt. 24:7
[210] See Lu. 21:11
[211] See Rom. 12:19
[212] Since the author has obtained some classical Greek education, these are likely to be Ireland and Britain, known since the time of Ptolemy's surveys.
[213] See Is. 45:7
[214] This is perhaps at least partially interpolated from how the texts renders 'the spirit of assistance'.

This is the term that is used elsewhere in the Gospel of John 14, where "the advocate" is discussed. However, it is not rendered as it is commonly in Ethiopian liturgy as 'menifesi k'idusi'.
[215] Perhaps alluding to the episode at Dan. 2:45-46
[216] 'lek'idusu'- the coming of someone notable, in this context, the return of Christ.

34:18 On that day, all the people and all the children of Israel's deeds shall be scrutinized.

Chapter XXXV:
Judgment upon the Princes of Israel

35:1 The Lord is troubled by you because you did not render a true judgment for the orphan- Woe unto you princes of Israel!

35:2 Woe to those who enter a tavern by morning and by night so that they might be filled with drunkenness, who are weak in judgement and who do not hear the need of the widow or the orphan, and who abide in sin and fornication.

35:3 The Lord spoke to the princes of Israel saying, "Unless you have abided by My commands, keeping My law, and loving what I love, woe unto you" [The Lord] said.

35:4 I shall bring down my wrath upon you, full of tribulation and punishment; you will perish and become food for the beetles and the moths. Your roads and your territories will be lost," He said to them.

35:5 Your nations will become a wilderness. All those people who behold her previously will clap their hands. They will gaze upon this sight and say "Was this not the nation filled in its great bounty and those people who loved it? The Lord has done this because of the sin of its denizens.

35:6 They will say, "[This nation] became proud, exalting herself and becoming blind to the truth until the Lord devastated her [inhabitants] upon the earth. She shall, therefore, become a barren wasteland because of the conceit of those who dwelled within her. Thorns have grown out onto the thistles, woe to her!

35:7 Weeds and nettles grow forth from her land, for she is barren and desolate. Wild beasts reside within her."

35:8 The judgment of the Lord has been cast upon her. She will drink from the cup of the Lord's judgment because of the great and sinful arrogance of her inhabitants; and she will, consequently, become a place of terror to all those who attempt to approach her.

Chapter XXXVI:
Promises made because of the Fidelity of Abraham[217]

36:1 Macedonians, do not boast[218], Amalekites, do not grow stubborn, for the Lord is He who shall lay waste to you.

36:2 (For in your grandiosity will ascend to the heavens), only thereafter, you will be cast down into Gehenna.

36:3 In the past, when Israel left the land of Egypt and went into the kingdoms of Moab and Midian, [Moses] said, "Do not be too proud, for it is not for us to claim what rightly belongs to the Lord."[219]

[217] This appears to be an independent sermon that is unrelated to the content of the prior chapters.

[218] Plutarch reports this as a common ethnic vice attributed to Macedonians in antiquity.
[219] See Ps. 113:9

36:4 You, the people of Ishmael[220], child of the slave, why do you act stingy for things besides money? Do you not think that the Lord will not cast judgment at his appointed time when He arises to render his verdict upon the earth?

36:5 The Lord, the ruler of the universe, said, "Soon you will receive the tribulation that you have wrought by the work of your hands. Why do you hold such high regard for your rational? Why do you harden your hearts?

36:6 I will hold tight to your lofty claims against me, just as you spoke them to the alien in your land. For you do only as you wish, which merits only sin. [Therefore], I will ignore you while you abide in the land to which you were sent."

36:7 The Lord, the ruler of the world, has said "I shall cast this upon you". He said, "Yet, if you are committed to moral deeds, and love those things which are precious to me, I will listen to all of your pleas and supplications.

36:8 If you do My will, I will protect your wishes, shielding you from your enemy and blessing your many descendants and all of your seed.

36:9 I will make your herds of cattle and sheep abound for your behalf, if you abide by the commandments and if you hold close to your heart all that is beloved to Me." The Lord, the King of the universe spoke, "I will offer My benediction to you and all that you possess."

36:10 "Yet, if you do not follow My will, if you do not abide in the law I have given to you, the wrath that you have heard of in former days will descend for you. Since you did not observe my law or abide by My commandments, you cannot escape from the wrath that will fall upon you.

36:11 I am your God, who imparted you with life, yet you have not respected what is precious to Me.

36:12 All of this was your treasure, set aside so that you may kill and reconcile, that you might build and demolish, that you might dole out honor and abuse, that might raise and cast down. Yet, you have abandoned My worship and praise, though I was He who imparted you with sovereignty, as well as the dignity to reign with authority upon those below you. You will not escape from My wrath that I will cast upon you.

36:13 If you had done the will of the Lord, and abided by His commandments, He would show his love to you. Together you might rejoice in his sovereignty and might be kin to those who shall inherit the promised land.

36:14 For He has said, "Those who properly abide, I will grant them prestige and show them the fullness of my love. I will make them rejoice in the Temple[221] where they pray." The Lord, the King of the universe, has said, "They shall be [My] beloved, [My] elect, because of their sacrifices.

[220] The only direct address to arab people in this text, which appears to only be concerned with their financial acumen.

[221] Pressumably the Jerusalem Temple

36:15 Do not avoid considering the state of others, and act in righteousness, so that you might cross from death into life.

36:16 The Lord shall protect all those men who do moral deeds that they might be His servants, just as the Lord protected Job in his ordeal.

36:17 The Lord will protect all those who are committed to righteousness, that they are to be His servants just as Abraham was. For He saved [Abraham] when he killed the kings[222]. Or, Moses, who He saved from the hand of the Canaanites and the Pharaoh, where Abraham had resided. [The Canaanites] harassed him, dawn until dusk, demanding that he might worship their idols.

36:18 When they brought him before the idols that were their treasure, he still refused and endured their mocking.

36:19 Abraham had faith in [the Lord] from his youth, and the Lord trusted him as a friend. [Therefore, Abraham] refused them, as he would only worship his Creator, the Lord.

36:20 Because of his love for the Lord, he did not stop his praise of Him until he passed away. He never deviated from His law, all the days of his life. He also taught his children to observe the law of the Lord.

36:21 Just as their father Abraham kept His law, they did not depart from the law of the Lord. For [the Lord] said unto the angels, "I have a helper in this world named Abraham."

The children of Abraham, Isaac and Jacob, are His servants as the Lord spoke to them and they did not deviate from His law.

36:22 The Lord, whom they praised, and who is ruler of all things, spoke, saying "Abraham is My companion, Isaac is My confidant, and Jacob is the friend who is precious to My heart."

36:23 In the age when He loved the children of Israel, they resided with Him while they made Him grieve. Yet, he tolerated this, feeding them manna while they were in the wilderness.

36:24 Their clothes did not become worn, since they had been fed manna, that is the bread[223] of knowledge[224], and they did not have to march.

36:25 Yet, their hearts were distant from the Lord forever, as those who have committed sin in ancient days have no hope for salvation.

36:26 They became as a crooked bow. They did not walk in the ways of their fathers: Isaac, Abraham and Jacob, who had served the Lord in their good life. They would offend Him, repeatedly, upon the mountains and highlands, with their idols. They would gorge themselves in those mountain and caves upon tree roots.

36:27 They slaughtered a heifer as a sacrifice, being full of conceit because of the work of their hands. They would eat and drink of their sacrifice, entertaining demons with their song.

---

[222] See Gen. 14:1-17
[223] 'mit'adi'- an Ethiopian bread made from wheat flour.

[224] This is intented to parallel the Christian doctrine of the Eucharist, wherein the bread that is consumed if from the freely given grace of God. See Jn. 6:35

36:28 The demons had great admiration for their songs and amusement. They would commit themselves to drunkenness and adultery without restraint, and thought to rob and be consumed by gluttony, which is reprehensible to the Lord.

36:29 For the idols of Canaan and for the idols of Midian, the idols Baal, Apis[225], Dagon, Serapis[226], and Artemis[227], who are Philistine idols.

36:30 As for all the idols of the people who reside in that land, they would make sacrifices to them; and Israel would worship those idols, just as the people worship the wealth that they have seen and heard. They would offer games and songs to them and make a great noise on their behalf.

36:31 All of the people of Israel do the same, saying "We will worship the Lord, but not observe his commandments or the law given to us by Moses." The law of the Lord was given to them so that they might observe it and be strangers to the worship of idols.

36:32 [He looked] to prevent them from worshipping idols, beyond that of their father's God, who nourished them on honey and manna, on harvested grain and who has sent forth the bounty of the earth.

36:33 Moses charged them, saying "Do not worship them! For the Lord is your God and He feeds those who love Him. He will not neglect those who love Him and chose Him."[228]

36:34 Despite this, they did not stop in their offenses against the Lord. They would grieve the Lord while He gave them reasons to rejoice.

36:35 When [the Lord] would make them downtrodden, they would cry to Him and He would spare them of the tribulation that they had received. For this they would again rejoice and abide like this for the epoch.

36:36 However, in later days they would again turn their hearts to sin, offending the Lord just as they had done previously. He would, therefore, send in alien nations to destroy them, who would subjugate and tax them[229].

36:37 Again, they would turn towards their God, the Lord, and weep.

36:38 Yet, He would still grant them forgiveness. It is because of their fathers: Noah, Isaac, Abraham and Jacob, all of whom served the Lord in their life, from youth to old age. It is not for their sake that He grants forgiveness to them, but because of the oath[230] He had taken.

---

[225] An Egyptian bull deity popular in North Egypt. His cult survived until the late 4ᵗʰ century when it was banned by the Edict of Thesalonica.
[226] A Hellenic-Egyptian deity, which combined the Apis bull and Osirus. Its popular was at its height in the Ptolemaic period, but survived until the late 4ᵗʰ century AD. The Coptic Patriarch held particular disdain for this idol, leading a mob to destroy it in Alexandira in 389.
[227] An exceedingly common Greek deity, albeit unusual in Africa. She may be known to the author as she is mentioned in Acts 19:35.
[228] See Ex. 16:3-4
[229] Since taxation is only introduced in the Levant in the 10ᵗʰ century BC, the author can only be referencing the latter political powers of: Babylon, Persia, Egypt, Rome and the Seleucid Empire. Rather then those political bodies which oppressed Israel prior to the establishment of its kingdom.
[230] See Gen. 22:16

36:39 He loves those who keep His law and will make their descendants increase like the stars in the sky and the sand in the sea[231].

36:40 One the day of the resurrection, all those who are as the sand in the sea are sinners, whose souls will be separated from the children of Israel and come into Gehenna.

36:41 For the Lord said to Abraham, "Look up to the heavens at night, and count the stars, if you were able to number them."[232] Thereafter, He said to him, "Your children and the pious will shine in the heavens as the stars do, for those born of Israel possess generous souls."

36:42 He again spoke to [Abraham], saying "Look towards the banks of the river and towards the sea, look among the sands. Count them if you can. Your sinning children will be likewise, those who will descend into Gehenna at the day of resurrection. They are the souls of the sinful."

36:43 Abraham had trust in the Lord, and because of this he was faithful. He walked in confidence about the world; and when his elderly wife Sarah gave birth to a child, he was called 'Isaac'[233].

36:44 He believe that those who are committed to good deeds shall rise again and abide forever in the Kingdom of Heaven. Just as he too shall reside in the Kingdom of Heaven.

36:45 He had faith that all those who have been sinful shall descend into Gehenna and reside in that place forever after the resurrection of the dead. While those who were righteous in their deeds shall reign with [the Lord] eternally.

36:46 And he again believed that the eternal judgment to be passed would be just upon those who were committed to sin, and that he shall find the Kingdom of Life in heaven.

May the Lord be praised and glorified without deceit. The first book that recounts the acts of the Meqabyans is completed[234].

---

[231] See Gen. 22:17
[232] See Gen. 15:5
[233] See Gen. 21:5

[234] This seems to be a later addition to the text once it was compiled with the two additional books into a single codecies as a means of differentiating between them.

www.ingramcontent.com/pod-product-compliance
Lightning Source LLC
Chambersburg PA
CBHW070940120626
46546CB00004B/1487